Marianne Moore

Revised Edition

Twayne's United States Authors Series

Kenneth E. Eble, Editor

University of Utah

TUSAS 54

MARIANNE MOORE, *1938, by Arthur Steiner.*
The Rosenbach Museum & Library, Philadelphia.

Marianne Moore

Revised Edition

By Bernard F. Engel

Michigan State University

Twayne Publishers
A Division of G. K. Hall & Co. • *Boston*

Marianne Moore, Revised Edition
Bernard F. Engel

Copyright 1989 by G. K. Hall & Co.
All rights reserved.
Published by Twayne Publishers
A Division of G. K. Hall & Co.
70 Lincoln Street
Boston, Massachusetts 02111

Copyediting supervised by Barbara Sutton
Book production by John Amburg
Book design by Barbara Anderson

Typeset in 11 pt. Garamond
by Modern Graphics, Inc., Weymouth, Massachusetts

Printed on permanent/durable acid-free paper
and bound in the United States of America.

Library of Congress Cataloging-in-Publication Data

Engel, Bernard F.
  Marianne Moore / by Bernard F. Engel—Rev. ed.
    p.   cm.—(Twayne's United States authors series ; TUSAS 54)
  Bibliography: p.
  Includes index.
  ISBN 0–8057–7525–0
  1. Moore, Marianne, 1887–1972—Criticism and interpretation.
I. Title. II. Series.
PS3525.05616Z65   1988
811'.52—dc19   88–19157
                                                                    CIP

To Adele, wife and partner

Contents

About the Author

Bernard F. Engel has published a dozen books, among them the Twayne volume *Richard Eberhart*. He has also published more than 150 articles, notes, and reviews, most of them on American verse. Engel has been an admirer of Marianne Moore's verse since he was introduced to it as a student at the University of Oregon, where he earned his B.A. in 1946 after having served three years in the U.S. Army in World War II. In 1957, following some years in newspaper work and after earning additional degrees in English from the University of Chicago and the University of California at Berkeley, Engel joined the faculty of the Department of American Thought and Language at Michigan State University.

Preface

Two developments in the study of Marianne Moore's work have made desirable a revision of this book that was first published in 1964. One advance is the availability of her papers: reading diaries, correspondence, drafts of poems, and other documents, which in her later years she kept tied in neat bundles, stacked waist-high around two walls of her bedroom. Since her death most of this material has been housed in the Rosenbach Museum & Library in Philadelphia; some of the correspondence is in the Beinecke Library at Yale University. A second change is the growing recognition by readers and scholars that Moore was not simply a preacher of conventional moralities, that she understood, indeed, the fact that we live in a world of flux where we meet not a readily comprehensible moral order but the irrational mixture of experiences she terms "confusion." She sought, therefore, not conformity to an order but illumination, the discovery of the invisible in the world of the visible.

In this revision changes appear on every page. The 1964 edition has been most useful for giving a suggested reading of each of the poems in the 1951 *Collected Poems* (I used the 1959 printing of that work). In this new edition I again propose a reading for each poem, but I now refer to *The Complete Poems of Marianne Moore*. This work, first published in 1967, was carefully edited—only a few minor changes were needed—by Clive Driver and Patricia Willis and republished in 1981. Willis edited *The Complete Prose of Marianne Moore* (1986), the source, except as may otherwise be noted, for discussion of Moore's prose. Other changes amend or correct readings, sometimes to incorporate new understanding on my own part, sometimes to present or comment on information from the "papers" or from what other readers have said. The 1964 book was the first such study of the work of this great writer whose poems at the time were considered too difficult for the general reader. Perhaps on the grounds that if Engel could read them anyone could, other books began to appear; production of books, articles, and dissertations about Marianne Moore has now become almost an industry. The poems have drawn astute readers. I admire their work, have profited from their readings, and have updated the bibliography to include them.

Moore had the advice of Ezra Pound that the order of presentation in a book of poems is important; and she had the aid of T. S. Eliot in establishing the order in both *Selected Poems* and the 1951 *Collected Poems*.[1] Because of these counselors' authority and because it seems most convenient for the reader, I have considered her poems in the order in which they appear in the 1981 edition.

Bernard F. Engel

Michigan State University

Acknowledgments

When I prepared the 1964 edition of this book, Moore was a warmly courteous hostess and gave sprightly, generous, and prompt answers to letters. Although she did see the manuscript, she was in no way responsible for the book's statements of fact or its opinions.

Work was supported by Michigan State University all-university research grants. Janet M. Agnew, head librarian of Bryn Mawr College, furnished copies of Moore's poetry that had appeared in student publications.

In preparing this revision, I have had courteous cooperation from everyone at the Rosenbach Museum & Library in Philadelphia where Moore's papers are held. Patricia C. Willis, the former curator of books and manuscripts there; Leslie A. Morris, her successor; and numerous staff members have been of great assistance. The photograph of Moore by Arthur Steiner was generously supplied by the Rosenbach Museum & Library.

I acknowledge permission to reprint material as follows:

Quotations from *The Complete Poems of Marianne Moore*, copyright © 1969 by Marianne Moore. All rights reserved. Reprinted by permission of Viking Penguin Inc.

Quotations from *The Complete Prose of Marianne Moore*, edited by Patricia C. Willis, copyright 1955 by Marianne Moore; renewed © 1983 by Lawrence E. Brinn and Louise Crane, executors of the estate of Marianne Moore. All rights reserved. Reprinted by permission of Viking Penguin Inc.

Permission to quote from unpublished letters, reading diaries, and other papers at the Rosenbach Museum & Library has been granted by Clive E. Driver, literary executor of the estate of Marianne Moore.

Chronology

1925   Receives Dial Award for 1924; five consecutive issues of the *Dial* laud her work, and she becomes acting editor beginning with the July issue. For next four years she is active with the magazine and publishes no verse of her own.

1926   Appointed editor of the *Dial*, beginning with July issue.

1929   Publication of the *Dial* ends with July issue; Moore leaves Manhattan for the Brooklyn apartment that would be her home until 1966. Begins career as freelance poet, book reviewer, writer of occasional articles.

1932   Helen Haire Levinson Prize signifies her return to prominence as active poet.

1935   *Selected Poems.*

1936   *The Pangolin and Other Verse.*

1941   *What Are Years?*

1944   *Nevertheless.*

1945   Guggenheim Fellowship in creative writing. Translator, with Elizabeth Mayer, of Adalbert Stifter's *Rock Crystal, A Christmas Tale.*

1946   Joint grant of $1,000 from American Academy of Arts and Letters and National Institute of Arts and Letters. Begins translation of La Fontaine's *Fables.*

1949   "A Face" published separately. First of sixteen honorary degrees, a Litt.D. from Wilson College.

1951   *Collected Poems.* Within next two years, receives National Book Award, Pulitzer Prize, and Bollingen Prize.

1954   *The Fables of La Fontaine.*

1955   *Predilections* (selected essays).

1956   *Like a Bulwark.*

1959   *O to Be a Dragon.*

1961   *A Marianne Moore Reader.*

1962   *The Absentee.*

1963   *Puss in Boots, The Sleeping Beauty,* and *Cinderella.*

1966   Moves to Manhattan, causing much comment in New York newspapers.

1967   *The Complete Poems of Marianne Moore.*

1969   Receives final honorary degree, from Harvard University.

1972   Dies 5 February.

1981   *The Complete Poems of Marianne Moore,* Definitive Edition.

1986   *The Complete Prose of Marianne Moore.*

Chapter One

Poet and Person

Fascination with paradox is the most immediately striking aspect of the verse of Marianne Moore. Her famous counsel in her famous poem "Poetry" that poets should present "imaginary gardens with real toads in them," should be "literalists of the imagination," bewilders the student as it bemuses the critic. This interest in the seemingly contradictory was often witty and, at times, playful (the garden is populated not with hummingbirds and butterflies but with "real toads"). But it was also profound. Paradox is the essence of her work because she wished to advocate a set of values, yet was aware that there is more "confusion" than order in this changing universe, that adherence to ethical principles enables one to survive, will provide a momentary stay against "confusion," but is not in itself a path to comprehension. For understanding, one must bring both "mind" and "imagination," must, as in "The Steeple-Jack," recognize the intermixture of hope and danger, stranded whales and mewing seagulls and semitropical plants that makes up our existence.

The values she advocated are those of a morality that, she told a *Partisan Review* symposium,[1] is "self-demonstrating." They are those values that inspire decency as a member of a community and—more emphasized—those that she believed lead to honor as an individual. They include courage, independence, responsibility, genuineness, and a certain ardor in the conduct of one's life. Presentation of this ethics was built into her work. Her subject matter was whatever is experienced, whether through the senses or by the imagination.

Moore worked in a tradition that respected inductive methods. This is the tradition of, for example, William Blake, who wrote that "To Generalize is to be an Idiot. To Particularize is the Alone Distinction of Merit," and that "Without Minute Neatness of Execution The Sublime cannot Exist!" Belief that the artist can cause transmutation of accumulated particulars into a sublimity that is more than the sum of its parts is a romantic faith linking Blake to

Ezra Pound, to William Carlos Williams, and of course to Marianne Moore.

Moore's preaching therefore was restrained. She sought to illustrate and prove her convictions by careful selection of exact details to realize the particularities of an object. This she believed would make her presentation convincing to the reader who, it was assumed, would not accept what our era calls a "mere" abstraction. In its focus upon the object her method paralleled principles of the objectivism sponsored by Louis Zukofsky in the 1920s. Zukofsky rejected the term *movement* for his activities, and these were so short-lived and, indeed, so informal that such a term for them would be grandiose. Though his objectivism was scarcely a new principle, it is worth recalling because it aroused theoretical consideration of practices employed by Wallace Stevens as well as by Moore. Zukofsky's own not-always-coherent remarks in *An "Objectivists" Anthology* (1932) defined the "objective" as that which is aimed at, and objective poetry thus is that which is "objectively perfect, inextricably the direction of historical and contemporary particulars"; he recommended Moore's poem "An Egyptian Pulled Glass Bottle in the Shape of a Fish" and her early book *Observations* as examples.

Though Moore used the rigorously perceived detail, she was even less limited than Williams and Stevens to the "thing"—to the data accessible to the senses. It is true that when writing of an apple, for example, she would try to give, as Williams put it admiringly in a *Dial* review (May 1925), "the hard and unaffected concept of the apple itself as an idea, then its edge to edge contact with the things which surround it." What surrounds it, however, is not only a world of orchards, but one of brilliantly imagined connections and connotations, a world where apple trees mingle with caterpillars and pangolins and glaciers, with courages and voracities and ironies.

Though, as Bonnie Costello puts it, Moore was a "factualist,"[2] she did not limit herself to the directly perceived. She had climbed partway up Mount Rainier in 1923 while visiting her brother at the Bremerton navy yard; yet her poem about the mountain, "The Octopus," draws its information largely from guidebooks and other written sources. The point is emphasized in an entry in her notebook for 1916–21: "Give me those long descriptions of house parties, those chapters made up of dinner conversations, of endless hunting scenes . . . not in real life but in the pages of Trollope." Moore's was the sort of literary imagination that would sacrifice some of the sweat and surprises of an actual climb and a real dinner party in order to get the views of one who had studied the matter or reflected on it brilliantly. She sought to give not reports or editorial comments, but imaginative representations that would make her world large—larger than the petty, the humdrum, and the merely self-centered: in this enlargement she was armoring herself against the failures and temptations that could lead to deficiency in comprehension.

To Moore, objects were important because they are or contain something more than the qualities of mere phenomena. Focus on the object was a process of expansion, a discarding of mundanities to release a spiritual self. Belief in the existence of a spiritual understructure to the world of appearances gave her confidence in the rightness of her devotion to presentation of the object. As she says in "He Digesteth Harde Yron," the power of the visible is "the invisible"; by specifying exact details the poet can "dramatize a/ meaning always missed / by the externalist." The object, the freshly perceived "thing," has power to suggest or convey meaning by being its exact self because its selfhood—when seen clearly—is not narrowed from but is expanded beyond its physical outlines. To find the self is not to discover an irreducible stone of true being hidden inside a mass of the irrelevant and false. It is rather to throw a stone into a pool: it is to note the rings of meaning that widen around and beyond the self when it is set in motion.

Concern with both ethics and "things" made Moore frequently a poet of the analogy: she presented the "thing" in order to suggest or assert a point of ethics. And even though meanings were to arise from the object, she was not averse to tucking a "moral" into a poem. Sometimes, both in such relatively early work as "The Jerboa" and "The Plumet Basilisk" and in such later pieces as "The Arctic Ox," she was so charmed by the creature she was presenting that the delight the poem communicates is in itself the chief conveyer of meaning. Even in these poems, however, there are bits of overt statement, significant juxtapositions, and other signposts for the reader.

But a poet so earnest in advocacy of values may also be expected to break into direct commentary, and this Moore sometimes did. To the critic who values metaphor in one form or another as the essence of poetry, her practice may seem too editorial. Roy Harvey Pearce, for example, in *The Continuity of American Poetry* doubts that such of her work as "What Are Years?" is poetry at all. Moore's admirers obviously believe that she succeeded in making commentary function as presentation, that she knew just how much delineation of the "thing" is needed to honey the lip of the cup.

Objectivity was one strategy enabling Moore to keep her eye on the object. Another tactic for adherence to the thing itself was restraint, what critics, recognizing a principle that biographers will no doubt see as meeting a psychological need, call her "armoring." She guarded against intrusion of conventional feeling: hence, for example, her frequent selection of exotic animals and other "things" about which the reader is not likely to have preconceptions. She wanted to avoid reference to her private life and, usually, to her own political and social opinions. Desire for such restraint demanded of her the self-sufficiency to explore fresh subject matter, and it reinforced her insistence on the self-discipline that would enable her to adhere to her subject.

Achievement of Distinction: Tactics of Style

The most obvious characteristic of Moore's style is discipline. In her best work she did not allow presentation to soar far from reference to a concrete object, whether animal, glass, or coral; no system of analogy, no overall metaphor, was permitted to assume governance, to lure the poem away from its particulars. In the early poem "Melanchthon" (first titled "Black Earth")—a piece unfortunately omitted from later collections—the rhetorical form is that of a series of questions, but by inversion and by careful placement these are subdued to avoid proselike obviousness. The poem's deliberate, declarative tone is further guarded by the use of seemingly subordinate *which* clauses to advance assertions and by the linking of series of statements with semicolons instead of with conjunctions to give an effect of factual assertion. Rhyme is present in the first two lines of each stanza, but is de-emphasized so as to avoid musicality; the meter, based on careful counting of syllables, also is intended to support the guise of reasoned statement.

The poem admits neither ungrounded interpretations of the aesthetic data nor obvious ornament. The desired effect is that of careful deliberation, serious but not grim, and conversational rather than flatly argumentative. The style, that is, exemplifies the restraint that Moore valued.

The rhetoric and style of "Melanchthon" are representative, but are by no means the only tactics Moore employed. She could vary from the editorial ("What Are Years?") to the celebratory ("The Jerboa," "The Plumet Basilisk") and the deliberately ponderous ("To a Steamroller"). She was nearly always witty and sometimes exploited devices of wit to develop an entire poem; examples are "For February 14th," depending on reversal of expectations, and "Carnegie Hall: Rescued," setting up a proposition in order to demolish it. In her meditative, exploratory mood she might, as in "Armor's Undermining Modesty," begin with seeming casualness and move by apparently whimsical juxtapositions to investigate calmly now one, now another aspect of her topic until she arrived at a strongly felt though sententious disclosure. When she would scold, she was more direct. Thus the rhetorical pattern of "Critics and Connoisseurs" is that of a series of assertions, each followed by an illustrative incident or a bit of evidence, the whole leading to the concluding edged question.

She indicated a liking for patterns in passages admiring the soaring of seagulls and pelican flocks, the careful craftsmanship of bottles and carriages. Her customary linking, within a poem, of materials drawn from a diversity of sources strengthens the impression that one of her aims was to discover and to present a unity within multiplicity. This belief helped account for incongruities of structure and wording, and these in turn allowed her to express the paradoxes of existence. Her ability deftly to relate bric-a-brac enabled her to come at a point from several angles and to avoid crude one-to-one comparisons. Though this probing of diversities often caused her to make abrupt juxtapositions and sudden shifts in syntax, she was careful not to let brilliance of individual lines overpower the poem. Indeed, just as she selected the conversational for use in quotations, so she avoided the trenchant aphorism in her own wording. Her wit was to inform the whole poem, not to give sparkle to individual lines.

Her frequent presentation of a long line followed by a shorter one could be used for the quick shifts in thought characteristic in poetry of wit, but she deliberately muted her statement. The line patterns do allow surprises, but these are typically caused by her associations of seemingly disparate objects nad insights, not by crisp or clever twists in argument. Disruptive clause placements serve to

quicken the pace and to suggest intellectual meditation as well as
to enable presentation of paradox.

Restraint in style caused her frequently to omit connectives and
to proceed from phase to phase of a poem by juxtaposition rather
than by obvious transition. This method forces the reader to stretch
his imagination—surely not an unhealthy form of exercise. If her
associative processes are sometimes hard to follow, rereading generally proves that the fault has been lack of sufficient flexibility on
the part of the reader. She was never cryptic because of private
symbolism or merely fashionable metaphor; in "Picking and Choosing" she reproaches the critic who, "daft about the meaning," is
fond of finding electric profundities in every simple candle. Restraint, she held, means that the poet commits herself and in return
has a right to expect the reader to use intelligence and imagination.

Moore's diction is usually unobtrusive, the "good" colloquial
English suited to the generally meditative and conversational tone
of her poems. Occasionally, as in "To a Steam Roller," she would
use Latinate vocabulary for philosophical reflections and short words
for physical description. A full study of her diction, however, would
disclose not a special poetic vocabulary but an interaction of ordinary
words designed to exploit connotations and to encourage expression
of paradox.

She did not always use rhyme, but when she did it could be
subdued and intricate. It was often unstressed, and, as with her wit
and metaphor, she would go to some lengths to assure that it did
not overpower argument. She maintained restraint not only by the
"feminine" rhyming of unstressed syllables but also by careful placing of words and phrases so that the word that ends in an unstressed
rhyme is itself in a de-emphasized position. Her early work was
famous for occasional breaking of words in the middle so that the
first syllable of a word might end a line and serve as a rhyme to
the eye, though not to the ear unless the reader chose to give it an
unusual stress. She often, but not always, revised her work in later
printings so as to avoid these unusual rhymes; the continued presence
of some of them demonstrates that she came to use fewer of them
not because she had developed an objection to the principle, but
because she felt that in their unusualness they might obtrude and
thus violate the governing principle of restraint.

Occasionally she would alter her handling of rhyme to create a
special effect, as in "To a Steam Roller" where rather more emphatic

rhyme than usual seems intended to suggest the solidity of the subject. Her willingness to experiment with rhyme was partly a device to make possible her use of highly disciplined metric.

In some of her early poems her line lengths were determined not by accentual-syllabic principles of conventional English metrics but by adhering to a precise syllable count, with the lines of one stanza parallel in length to the corresponding lines of the next one. Though French and Italian predecessors have been suggested for this custom, it seems more likely that Moore acquired it from the experimentalism of American verse in the pre–World War I years. Adelaide Crapsey, Mina Loy, and other women poets of that era wrote poems in syllabic verse, and many "new" poets experimented with rigorously controlled Japanese verse forms. Moore herself gave great importance to matters of verse technique; her expertise in it was one of the qualities T. S. Eliot found of high value in his introduction to her *Selected Poems*. For the general reader, her counting of syllables, careful parallelism of line lengths, and intricate use of rhyme all reinforce her emphases upon discipline and precision.

Restraint appears in a variety of other ways. She seldom opened a poem with a resounding declaration or with a startlingly vivid figure; she preferred an artfully casual beginning in order to maintain her conversational tone. She sometimes ended a poem with a statement cast as a negative, a device she apparently hoped would avoid flatness that might arise from direct, proselike assertion and also would support her desired restraint. In revisions she frequently sought to remove what seemed to her too obvious statements or intimations of proselike "meaning." For example, she cut from "The Buffalo" a passage making it obvious that she was writing of a print, and she deleted from late printings of "Nine Nectarines" words in the original title that made it apparent she was dealing with the illustration on a piece of porcelain.

Moore's use of notes and of quotations is also evidence of desire for discipline in assertion. As with Shelly's comments on "Queen Mab" and Eliot's notes to "The Waste Land," her notes are often not strictly necessary to an understanding of the poem. She was aware of this, and in *What Are Years* and—with slightly altered wording—in later collections she included "A Note on the Notes" suggesting that the reader who finds the notes obtrusive might "take probity on faith" and disregard them. They do demonstrate her desire to give credit to sources, but of more importance is their function as evidence. They remind one of Hawthorne's device for persuading his reader that his stories were true, his habit of remarking that events he told of really did happen. Moore had a similar desire to be taken as a truth-teller; hence her presentation of notes that, though unnecessary for anyone but the pedant, give an air of veracity. The notes to "Camellia Sabina," for example, are of interest in themselves but are scarcely enlightening for the reader of the poem; their function is to demonstrate that the odd and colorful materials are not merely imagined.

We scarcely need to know that the cat in "Peter" is the pet of two friends, but a note to tell us this helps verify what is apparent in the poem: this is a particular cat, not a representative of some general quality of catness. It adds to our comprehension of "O to Be a Dragon!" to know which of various possible symbolisms Moore has particular reference to, though even this poem is understandable without the citation. Sometimes her desire for precision causes her to let allusiveness become excessive: "Hometown Piece for Messrs. Alston and Reese," for example, is accessible only to the baseball fan or to the devoted reader willing to track down performances of now-retired players in forgotten games.

The quotations with which she filled her poems came from a multiplicity of sources: books of all sorts, newspapers, magazines, and speeches or conversations. She sometimes explained her use of quotations as simply a convenience, asking, as in the foreword to *A Marianne Moore Reader*, "When a thing has been said so well that it could not be said better, why paraphrase it?" It made her writing, she said, "a kind of collection of flies in amber." Actually her quotations were carefully selected to avoid the impression of a catalog of beauties; she quoted not the colorful or the aphoristic but the casual, not particularly artful remark that would contribute to the conversational tone. She also explained, in "A Note on the Notes," that her "hybrid method of composition" made it ethically necessary for her to cite sources for her quotations and, in *A Marianne Moore Reader*, she cited George Saintsbury as authority for the idea that direct quotation is the best method of exhibiting a personality.

The reader will notice that Moore, being an artist rather than a scholar, freely altered quotations to make them fit her syntax or ideas. He will also notice that she by no means always cited a source for a quotation. Thus the full versions of "Poetry" give William Butler Yeats as the source for her famous phrasing "literalists of the imagination," but the exact wording is her own; late printings enclose in quotation marks the poem's equally famous expression "imaginary gardens with real toads in them," but give no source for it. These considerations lead the reader to suspect that Moore often used quotation marks as a device of rhetoric rather than as an indication of borrowing.

Thus in the poem "Silence" she intended to keep herself at a slight remove from the material: putting most of the piece in quotation marks, as the *Complete Poems* printing does, enabled her to present an assertive editorial commentary without seeming merely didactic. (In *A Marianne Moore Reader* she achieved the same result, though putting only two lines in quotation marks, because she so handled the material as to make most of the rest of the lines seem an indirect quotation.) Together with the fact that she altered the wording of the quotation she cited as her source for the idea of the poem, these usages indicate that not scholarly accuracy but artistic presentation governed her use of quotation marks. Both notes and quotations are sometimes means of giving credit to sources; but more often they seem intended to subdue any impression of assertiveness, to suggest that responsibility for a bit of lore or a remark does not lie directly on the poet.

Another device for maintaining restraint in commentary was use of animals as subjects. Moore knew not only that we will recognize qualities and behaviors in animals akin to those of our human associates, but also that our awareness that a matter after all concerns "lower" creatures will enable us to save face while absorbing the lesson. Her use of an animal differed markedly from that of the fabulist, for though she presented her animal in action, she seldom involved it in a narrative. Moreover, she consistently used animals to represent desirable qualities; it is man who is guilty of greed, falseness, misuse, and other errors that she condemned. She did not commit a pathetic fallacy: because of her objectivism, her jerboa and pangolin and basilisk are clearly themselves, not men in little.

Her ideas on the relationship of man and animals are most fully illustrated in "The Pangolin," a poem showing that man, though he may draw lessons from animal behavior, has other and more profound responsibilities. She frequently wrote of exotic animals, partly to take advantage of the color and excitement of the unusual, but also to avoid stock associations—she did not want to weaken her presentation by relying on faithful dogs, sly foxes, and innocent sheep. The animal world, in addition, gave her a handy set of references, something the twentieth-century poet, unable to depend upon familiarity with classic myth or even with biblical allusions, often feels compelled to get along without. The exotic nature of some of her creatures is not a bar to communication, since it is easy to give a sufficient description. As we might expect, the animals she most often writes of are the self-sufficient who survive by disciplined behavior. She wrote in the foreword to *A Marianne Moore Reader* that the animal is an exemplar of art because of his naturalness. His self-discipline provides a useful lesson for errant man.

She had her idiosyncrasies. She occasionally experimented with punctuation marks, especially with colons and semicolons in "The Labors of Hercules" and "England"; her usages do not seem consistent. She changed from single to double quotation marks at nearly every printing, her preference perhaps depending upon the appearance of the marks in particular typefaces. She sometimes used as a title the first line of a poem; since this would cause the reader to read the words twice, she often left the title in the usual large type but counted it as the first line, so that what seems at first glance to be the opening line is actually the second. Her titles sometimes are functional in other respects also. The title of "Sun" makes it explicit that the sun is the object addressed in the poem; and one might have difficulty recognizing that refugees are the subject of "Rescue with Yul Brynner" were it not for the title's hint.

A Kind of Tame Excitement

Devotion to her poetic career—as well, perhaps, as desire for the armoring that "silence" affords—kept Moore from writing an autobiography. The idea occurred to her, of course. Pascal Covici of Viking Press assured her, she told me, that she would have to work only an hour and a half a day to produce an autobiography. But, she remarked, she could not work "that way": she thought always of whatever work she had in hand at the moment and preferred not to take on more than one task at a time. She was courteous to interviewers, supplied brief write-ups for biographical guidebooks, and published a few essays touching on aspects of her life.

She said that if her life story is written it will be a "very tame affair." It will be that if the biographer concentrates on the routine dates and dimensions of her life. Thousands of women have taught school and worked in a library, and many of them have lived the scarcely munificent life of a free-lance poet. Even editorship of the *Dial*, outstanding though Moore's conduct of it was, was hardly in itself a flamboyantly unusual activity for an American writer in the 1920s. An understanding of her talents must come from somewhere other than a résumé of her outward circumstances.

Moore was born in Kirkwood, Missouri, a suburb of St. Louis, on 15 November 1887, the second child of Mary and John Milton Moore. Her father, an engineer, had just suffered a nervous breakdown after failure of his plans to manufacture a smokeless furnace and had gone home to his parents in Portsmouth, Ohio. Mrs. Moore had consequently returned to the home of her father, the Reverend John Riddle Warner, a Scotch-Irish Presbyterian minister. Though the Reverend Warner met the Reverend Eliot at St. Louis clerical functions, the families of Moore and of T. S. Eliot, who was born in St. Louis ten months after Moore, were not socially acquainted.

Mrs. Moore remained in Kirkwood as her father's housekeeper until he died in 1894. She then took her two children—John was seventeen months older than Marianne—to Carlisle, Pennsylvania, where she lived on a small inheritance. For a time she was an English teacher at Carlisle's Metzger Institute, a school for girls that has since become a part of Dickinson College. The attachment of the three Moores to each other remained close. Mrs. Moore lived with Marianne until her death in 1947, and the poet, who dedicated *Collected Poems* to her, respected her mother's precision in language (she reported herself somewhat irritated, for example, by a reporter's misquotation that had her mother end a sentence with "around"). Her brother, John, made a career as a navy chaplain. Mother, son, and daughter kept up an extensive correspondence.

Moore attended the Metzger schools and entered Bryn Mawr College in Bryn Mawr, Pennsylvania, in 1905. There is perhaps exaggeration in her remark to *Current Biography* that she spent most of her time in the biology laboratory because she was too "immature" for the English and language courses she was interested in; she did publish a number of poems in the college literary magazines. One fellow student was Hilda Doolittle ("H.D."), who was later to help publish Moore's first book. After graduating with a bachelor of arts degree in 1909, Moore took a secretarial course at Carlisle Commercial College; and, for three and a half years, from 1911 to 1915, she taught stenography, typing, bookkeeping, commercial English, and commercial law at the United States Indian School in Carlisle. These subjects did not inspire her, she later told a *New Yorker* reporter; she would have preferred to stay home and read. Write-ups remark on the point that Jim Thorpe, the famous Indian athlete, took courses from her; always an admirer of the skilled and graceful, she told a *Newsweek* reporter that Thorpe was chivalrous and kind. As for herself, she said she was a poor teacher.

Meanwhile, her brother, John, after graduating from Yale, had been ordained a Presbyterian minister, and in 1916 was appointed pastor at the Ogden Memorial Church in Chatham, New Jersey, where Moore with her mother moved to keep house for him. But when America entered World War I, John joined the navy, and Marianne with her mother rented a basement apartment in Greenwich Village where they lived for eleven years.

In these second and third decades of the century Moore won recognition rather quickly as one of the leading spirits in the "new" poetry and, both because of her own creative work and because of her position on the *Dial,* became one of the best-known literary writers in America. Her professional publication began in 1915 when the *Egoist,* a London journal specializing in imagist verse, printed her "To the Soul of 'Progress' " (later "To Military Progress"). Moore was not an imagist, whatever that term may mean; she was of course acquainted with H.D., who had married Richard Aldington, writer and editor of the magazine. A month later, in May 1915, *Poetry* magazine published five of Moore's poems. Since Harriet Monroe, its founding editor, had made *Poetry* the leading journal for the new generation of American poets, this publication meant that Moore was recognized as one of the innovators.[3]

Through the World War I period and the early 1920s Moore's poems were printed in a variety of the "little" magazines which during these years appeared and disappeared with a rapidity paced to the uncertainties of their amateur publishers' checking accounts. One prominent little magazine enterpriser was Alfred Kreymborg, himself a poet, who associated with many of the "new" poets then working in the New York area, among them William Carlos Williams, Kenneth Burke, Wallace Stevens, Conrad Aiken, John Gould Fletcher, Richard Aldington, Mina Loy, and Moore. In *Troubador,* his autobiographical account of these years, Kreymborg reported that many of the group admired Moore—for her flaming red hair and her "mellifluous flow of polysyllables which held every man in awe" as well as for her poetry. He also said that John Marshall, a partner in New York's Little Bookshop Around the Corner, intended not long after 1915 to publish volumes of poetry by a number of new writers, including Moore as well as Williams, Stevens, Maxwell Bodenheim, Skip Cannell, and Kreymborg himself. One or more poems by Moore appeared in each of Kreymborg's annual *Others* anthologies of new verse for the years 1916, 1917, and 1919. Ezra Pound's early recognition of Moore's talents is indicated in his published letters. He wrote to Harriet Monroe in May 1915, praising Moore's titles, and by 1918 he was remarking that Moore, together with Williams and Mina Loy, was a central figure in discussion of poetry. Williams too was an early friend. Though in his *Autobiography* he speculates that he may have "brushed against" Moore when he visited girls at Bryn Mawr, his association with her appears to have begun when he helped Kreymborg edit the journal *Others*. Frequent references to her in his *Autobiography* and in his *Selected Letters* indicate that he and Moore shared in their group's feeling that they were engaged in an important cultural enterprise. Like Kreymborg, Williams speaks of Moore's red hair, imaginative conversation, and effect of innocence. "Marianne was our saint," he wrote. "Everyone loved her." Williams's letters also demonstrate his professional respect for her; they show him asking her advice and commenting upon her opinions with the seriousness of a fellow craftsman. (She, somewhat in contrast, seemed from the beginning of their relationship to have regarded both his subject matter and his less-disciplined verse as gross, even though at times she praised its freedom.)

After moving to New York, Moore worked for a time as a tutor. But she frequented the Hudson Park branch of the New York Public Library, where in 1921 she was given a part-time job as an assistant at a salary of fifty dollars a month. She told a *Newsweek* reporter in 1951 that she was not much of an asset there because she could never find anything; as with her derogation of her own teaching at Carlisle, this comment is possibly more accurate as an indication of modesty than as a report of fact.

Her first book publication came in 1921. Without Moore's knowledge, Winifred Ellerman (known under the pen-name Bryher and then the wife of Robert McAlmon), and H.D., both of whom had been associated with the imagists, had *Poems* brought out under the imprint of The Egoist Press. A note in Moore's second book,

Observations (1924), says that the *Poems* "collection" was "made and arranged by H.D. and Mr. and Mrs. Robert McAlmon." This statement was later reported in *Twentieth Century Authors;* in the supplement to that publication Moore said that the work was the effort of Bryher and H.D., Robert McAlmon not being involved. All twenty-four of the works in *Poems* had appeared in magazines.

Into the early 1920s Moore had a high reputation within the avant-garde but no fame among the broader group of Americans with cultural interests. Wide recognition came through her association with the *Dial*. This journal had been "re-established," as Moore put it in a retrospective *Partisan Review* essay, in New York in 1920 after a varied, often distinguished career in Chicago and a short tenure under other management in New York. Now it was taken over by two well-to-do backers, Scofield Thayer and Dr. J. S. Watson, who sought to print what an announcement in the June 1925 issue called "works of merit not welcomed by commercial magazines."

Abandoning the social emphasis of the magazine's former publishers, the new backers turned it into a periodical of the arts that functioned through the 1920s as the most vigorous, most highly regarded of American journals of culture. It was renowned not only for its literature but also for its commentary on music, drama, and fine arts, and for its photographs of paintings and sculpture. Its international luster is indicated by a sampling of its contributors. The November 1924 issue, for example, had contributions from Moore ("Sea Unicorns and Land Unicorns"), Kenneth Burke, Marc Chagall (a color photograph of a painting), Oswald Spengler, James Stephens, Jules Romains, Thomas Mann, and Edmund Wilson. Moore was the first of her group to win publication in the *Dial*. According to Kreymborg, she was asked to submit her work after she read her poem "England" at a party one night in 1920. The *Dial*, though "little" enough compared with the mass-circulation magazines, was already much better known and more stable than most literary periodicals; thus Moore's poems reached a sizable audience. From then on, her work appeared in it frequently.

Direct association with the *Dial* followed publication of Moore's second book *Observations,* her first to appear in this country. By 1924 Williams was writing from Paris to report that Robert McAlmon wanted to publish a book of her work; Williams himself wanted to write a preface for it. *Observations* appeared in late 1924, however, as a publication of the Dial Press without direct aid from Williams. It incorporated all but three of the pieces earlier published in *Poems* and added several others. Its title was meant to suggest that the contents were both perceptions and commentaries; it made use of what was at the time a fashionable word (for example, T. S. Eliot's first book title: *Prufrock and Other Observations*).

This book was a milestone in Moore's public career, winning recognition that would be surpassed only by that given *Collected Poems*. The *Dial's* founders had established a cash award of two thousand dollars (not a "prize," as Moore explains in her essay on the magazine) for achievement in poetry; the first award had been made to Eliot in 1922. The award for 1924 was given to Moore. It was doubtless welcome for its cash as well as for its recognition. Pound's letters during the early 1920s suggested raising money to enable American poets, including Moore, to spend time in Europe; they also suggested her to the Guggenheim Foundation for an award. Poetry is not in our century a money-making endeavor.

The award led in turn to an annus mirabilis in the pages of the *Dial,* for five consecutive issues now carried tributes to her work. Glenway Wescott opened the parade with a general article in the January 1925 issue; the unsigned "Comment" columns of February, March, and April praised her; and Williams reviewed *Observations* in May. This accumulated recognition, together with the journal's frequent publication of her poems and reviews, made it scarcely surprising to readers of the June "Announcement" that, upon the resignation of Alyse Gregory as managing editor and the decision of Scofield Thayer himself to withdraw from active editing, Moore was appointed acting editor beginning with the July 1925 issue. The statement explained that Moore would actively assist Dr. Watson in choosing the contents of the magazine and would exercise the publication chores until now performed by the managing editor; Thayer himself and Dr. Watson were to continue to appoint the magazine's correspondents, select the Dial Award recipient, and choose the frontispiece. A year later, however, the June 1926 issue announced that Thayer was resigning and that Moore had been named editor. From this point until appearance of the final issue in July 1929, Moore was actively engaged in the day-to-day editing, correspondence, and publication details of the nation's most prominent journal of arts.

Proof of her success was the continued high reputation of the magazine, testified to by such diverse commentators as Frederick Hoffman ("the editorial sensibility of the decade," he wrote of her in *The Twenties*), e. e. cummings (lack of greater recognition of the periodical is owing to a "conspiracy" of "intellectual gangsters," he said in *Six Nonlectures*), and *Newsweek* (the journal fixed most presently established literary reputations, it said in 1951).[4]

There were, of course, some private and public detractors. Gorham B. Munson in *Destinations* accused Moore of lacking "impartial free intelligence," and she herself told Donald Hall in an interview (in *A Marianne Moore Reader*) of Hart Crane's quarrels with her editing. Others thought the *Dial* rather guarded than advanced. Bernard Smith, a Marxist, in his *Forces in American Criticism* found it, as might be expected, too "esthetic." The *New Republic* in 1927 made the astounding accusation that the *Dial* had not introduced a single new American writer of interest (an unsigned "Comment" column in the *Dial* gave the deft reply that the interest was in writing, not in writers). Even Williams, though exempting Moore from his condemnation, by 1928 was writing in letters that he was "disgusted" with what he thought were the magazine's "half-hearted ways" and "worthlessness"; since he did not specify his dislikes, we may assume that it no longer was novel enough for him.

Important as was her contribution to American letters as the *Dial*'s editor, Moore's real career was in poetry. But she had little time for writing while editing the magazine: Craig C. Abbott's bibliography of her work lists no verse from 1925 to 1932. When, in 1929, Dr. Watson gave up his interest to return to his home in Rochester, New York, Moore alone of the magazine's chief spirits remained. The announcement of the end of publication was an abrupt note at the end of the July issue, initialed by Dr. Watson. Moore's essay on the *Dial* was in a vein of celebratory, nostalgic reminiscence, kept from false sentiment by freshness of perception.

The change in her public career was matched by one perhaps equally important in her private life. Her mother had become ill, and her brother John was stationed at the Brooklyn Navy Yard. It seemed convenient for the women to move from their Greenwich Village basement apartment to Brooklyn's Cumberland Street and into the fifth-floor apartment where Moore lived until 1966. Here she spent an active three decades as free-lance poet, book reviewer, and article writer, continuing upon occasion to serve the cause of "new" poetry.

After the hiatus of the years on the *Dial,* she resumed publication of her verse. By 1934 a decade had passed since she had last put together a book. Apparently her friends were urging her to publish one; Elizabeth Sergeant reports (in *Robert Frost: The Trial by Existence*) that Frost was one of those offering to help. But arrangements were already being made for *Selected Poems,* which was brought out in 1935 by Macmillan in America and by Faber and Faber in England. This volume reprinted, often with alterations, most of the pieces published in *Poems* and *Observations,* and a number of others from magazines. Adoption by a commercial publisher gave the work relatively wide distribution, the new was no longer shocking, the *Dial* had given her an established reputation, and the book had an introduction by Eliot; for all these reasons, *Selected Poems* became primary in considerations of her work.

She published short books at intervals over the next fifteen years. *The Pangolin and Other Verse* (1936) printed five poems; some of these were among the fifteen published in 1941 under the title *What Are Years.* Six more appeared in *Nevertheless* (1944); and the poem "A Face" was published separately in 1949. She brought these publications together in *Collected Poems* (1951). Her translation of La Fontaine's *Fables,* begun in the mid-1940s, was published in 1954. She continued to win prizes—the Shelley Memorial Award in 1940, the Contemporary Poetry's Patrons' Prize and the Harriet Monroe Poetry Award in 1944, a Guggenheim Fellowship in 1945, and a joint grant from the American Academy of Arts and Letters and the National Institute of Arts and Letters in 1946. She taught composition at Cummington School, Massachusetts, in 1942, beginning a career as an occasional academician that would take her to poetry seminars, reading sessions, and lectureships at such schools as Bryn Mawr, Vassar, California (both in Berkeley and in Los Angeles), and Harvard. In 1949 she received the first of what was to become a long string of honorary degrees, a *litterarum doctor* from Wilson College, Chambersburg, Pennsylvania.

Publication of *Collected Poems* brought her a second annus mirabilis—the Pulitzer Prize, the National Book Award, and the Bollingen Prize. This work even established Moore as something of a celebrity. Her fame is indicated by a *New Yorker* magazine interview that makes much of her status as a Brooklynite, a *Newsweek* article illustrated with a small picture of her and a large one of Jim Thorpe, and the ultimate accolade of "*Life* Goes on a Zoo Tour with a Famous

Poet." Small wonder that in 1955 and 1956, when Ford Motor
Company was launching a new model, it called upon Moore to
suggest a name. Could the quick failure of the venture be punishment for the company's decision to use, instead of one of Moore's
suggestions, the family appellation Edsel? In the later 1950s and
1960s Moore's work was appearing even in such magazines as *Vogue*
and *Harper's Bazaar,* doubtless puzzling those who stumbled across
it while thumbing through the fashion advertisements. Meanwhile,
she brought out *Gedichte* (1954), a bilingual choice of her work;
Selected Fables (1955); *Predilections* (1955), a selection of her essays
and reviews; new poems in *Like a Bulwark* (1956) and *O to Be a
Dragon* (1959); *A Marianne Moore Reader* (1961), a miscellany of
poems and prose; and *The Absentee* (1962), a dramatized retelling of
Maria Edgeworth's prose story. She continued to publish verse in
magazines, brought out *Tell Me, Tell Me* in 1966, and edited the
1967 edition of *Complete Poems.*

The Poet at Home

She wrote proudly of her city's advantages for the imaginatively
curious; she says in her essay "Brooklyn from Clinton Hill" that it
afforded her "the kind of tame excitement on which I thrive." The
neighborhood was typical of miles of Brooklyn residential areas. Its
streets were lined with old three-story, red brick homes, many of
them housing two families. The population was mixed black, Puerto
Rican, and Caucasian. Most houses were built wall-to-wall and close
to the sidewalk, so that the yard areas were only patches of perhaps
five feet by ten. In some cases there was grass in this patch; at least
as often, it was bare dirt with a garbage can or two and perhaps a
tethered dog. On a sunny spring afternoon the streets were busy
with playing children, strolling dog-walkers, and honking auto-
mobiles; house-dressed women idled in their windows, calling to
each other or watching the life of the sidewalks. Though poor by
the standards of suburbia, the neighborhood was not what New
Yorkers would consider a slum. It offered an active, colorful multiplicity that was doubtless attractive to a poet whose real occupation
was observation.

Moore's own home was an apartment in a once-yellow, later gray
stone building, narrow enough and, at five stories, low enough to
be inconspicuous behind the trees whose leaves shaded it in the

summer. It had a touch of old-time elegance in the two "mothballs" (Moore's term for them)—white globes set on low black stands on either side of the front door. Moore lived on the top floor. Entering her apartment, one passed down a longish hallway lined with shelves of books and bric-a-brac (including a foot-square picture of a porcupine). The hall went past her bedroom, where a dresser and low shelves around the walls held a waist-high pile of manila envelopes of correspondence and the wall decorations included pictures of classic scenes like those that used to illustrate high school Latin books. The living room/dining room areas continued the impression of a place for comfortable living. At one end of the living room was a large table on which sat an old clock with a floral front; in this room also were two or three comfortable chairs, a variety of end tables, books on shelves and tables. There was a view of trees and streets, though a black iron fire escape edged down outside one window. The setting had the look of the well-worn, and in work areas was efficient but not fussy. Moore took the furnishings with her when she moved to Manhattan in 1966. After her death, a duplicate of the Manhattan living room was set up in the Rosenbach Museum & Library. (This room seems a good reproduction, though most of the dozens of small glass animals Moore had acquired on her own or from well-wishers have disappeared.)

Moore would meet a visitor at the door with a firm handshake and ask if he had found the elevator, a question she would come back to, as she had been distressed by the sight of friends puffing their way up the stairs. She was a slender, blue-eyed woman of medium height who put on glasses to read and wore her hair— once red, by the 1960s gray to white—looped in a long coil around the top of her head. She would seat her guest, serve orange juice and crackers, and, when she first sat down, would seem to withdraw slightly as if to brace herself for an ordeal. But in conversation she would become animated, moving from topic to topic in a series of juxtapositions reminiscent of the technique of her poetry. In one three- or four-minute burst she could leap from praise of a scholar in English from Belgrade to commendation of a dramatic version of E. M. Forster's *A Passage to India,* then to her enjoyment of a lecture by Thornton Wilder, and to favorable remarks about Theodore Roethke's teaching in Seattle; on to praise of Karl Barth; and finally to mention of criticism of her writing at Bryn Mawr (an instructor told her she hid her point in writing; but, she would say, "I survived it"). All this she knit together, in this instance the theme being the need for clearness in expression.

She would give anecdotes of other writers, but only if assured that her auditor would not pass them on because she would not "denigrate" anyone in public. Because Hemingway had only recently died, I did not in the first edition of this book publish statements about him she made to me in 1962. She told me then, with anger in voice and complexion, that Hemingway had been drunk when he called her up one night to complain about her rejection of his submissions to the *Dial* (it was the drunkenness, not the complaint, that irked her), and that when Wallace Stevens accepted Hemingway's dinner invitation in Florida he was "shocked" to discover that the novelist had picked up a couple of women in a bar to spend the evening with them. The desire to avoid catty gossip is admirable; the fact that Moore could still feel anger decades after the events shows that she was as human as the rest of us. Laudatory remarks by William Carlos Williams, and Moore's austere way of life and her advocacy of moralisms, have created an impression of saintliness that it suited her to project. Understanding would be furthered with more recognition that though she had considerable virtues she was not a plaster saint.

Celebrity had its costs. Moore regretted the need to spend her morning hours keeping up with correspondence, much of it from writers of term papers. She met requests politely, but could not give much time to them. She also complained that people asked her for photographs. Spoiled in their expectations by accounts of motion picture stars who had studio publicity budgets, readers made great demands on the energy and funds of a poet who had neither private wealth nor extensive commercial support. In her attempts to be helpful, she told me, she had stumbled "into all kinds of predicaments." She added: "I am not suspicious; I do not hate people; I do get taken in quite often." Certainly in her reception of a visitor Moore was solicitous and helpful. She would show a passage from a work in progress, exhibit proofs of a poem about to be printed, check on the level of orange juice in the glass, apologize for a smell of floor cleaner in the hallway (though praising the cleaning woman for her effort), ask whether her guest smoked and admire him for having quit, and on his departure urgently remind him of the elevator.

Her move to an apartment in Manhattan in 1966 drew front-page attention in the *New York Times.* Moore refused to give reasons for the move; press speculation suggested that she had come to fear crime in the old neighborhood. She remained a public figure, honored by the mayor and even throwing out the first ball at the 1968 baseball season opener at Yankee Stadium. Illness limited her activities in her last years, but her death on 5 February 1972 was reported on the front page of the *Times.*

Chapter Two

The Armored Self:
Selected Poems

Moore's strategies and emphases changed, but there is a consistency throughout her work. She believed that behavior and aesthetic practice should follow the same principles and that both should be based on a perception of "rock crystal" reality. This reality shows that our world is one whose multiple appearances must be recognized but must not be allowed to obscure unity of spirit and matter. Her poetry is a continual meditation upon this point and upon the consequent necessities in human behavior. People live in an environment containing both comfort and peril; the ideal for human performance is heroism. The characteristics of heroism include genuineness, courage, self-discipline, and ability to perceive reality. One must be aware of mystery but not therefore be esoteric, must admit complexity but retain clarity and spontaneity, must value restraint and art but not thereby lose ardor.

Heroism is needed in this world where the very ocean is a grave. The poem is an imaginative act, an effort, as Costello puts it, "to reconstruct the world in language."[1] Moore's famous armoring was psychological as well as professional. One may note her comment to Bryher, who, together with H.D., had achieved publication of Moore's first book, *Poems* (1921). Thanking Bryher, Moore wrote to her on 27 July 1921 that she now had "no place to hide." The rueful humor is revelatory. Moore's reticence was a part of her shield against the world, a shield that biographers will no doubt see as needed for reasons of her own being, as well as for aesthetic security.

Because differences in method and approach do develop, one may conveniently divide her work into periods, with the first of these culminating in *Selected Poems*.

Rock Crystal Things to See

Selected Poems (1935) incorporates—frequently with minor alterations and sometimes with major revisions—most of the works published in *Poems* and in *Observations* (1924), and most of her other verse of the 1920s and early 1930s. With further revisions, the 1935 volume is reprinted as the opening section of *Complete Poems* (1981).

The opening two poems are portions of a piece originally printed in 1932 with three sections under the heading "Part of a Novel, Part of a Poem, Part of a Play"; the individual sections were headed "The Steeple-Jack," "The Student," and "The Hero." (Moore omitted "The Student" from the 1951 collection, but restored it in later books. In the 1981 collection it appears as a separate poem, almost 100 pages after the other two pieces. This discussion therefore will deal with it separately.)

The "confusion" that exists in the seemingly placid environment of an ordinary town is examined in "The Steeple-Jack." The town, which represents the environment of most human lives, is calm, seemingly well ordered. Yet we remember that to be human is to face death—an inevitability Moore neither grows lyrical over like Whitman nor rages against like Dylan Thomas but accepts as part of reality. The first four stanzas, which picture the setting, open with the remark that the scene would have appealed to Albrecht Dürer, the German Renaissance artist. The reader is to recognize that Dürer is famed for placing apocalyptic visions in everyday settings. The poem presents the town on a "fine day" when there are "formal" waves on the water, an orderly flock of seagulls lazily circling the spires, water changing color in definite bands, and fishermen who have carefully spread their nets for drying. Yet this scene is not entirely tidy: on the beach are eight stranded whales (mention of an exact number adds to the impression of precision); the gulls, though steady, nevertheless quiver slightly; and, we are reminded, when storms come they put in disarray both grass and stars. (We may also recall that in one of her best-known poems, "A Grave," Moore has the sea function as a deceptive peril to man.) The words of the fourth stanza, "it is a privilege to see so / much confusion," sum up the appearance of the scene and the poet's attitude that a view of it is revelatory.

The last four stanzas present a specific example of the "confusion" noted in the town's general aspect and find a unity in the apparent variety. A steeple-jack in red, the color of warning, leaves a danger sign on the sidewalk while he gilds the star on a church spire. This little scene in itself constitutes one of the paradoxes of which Moore

was fond. She delighted in such discoveries because they apparently
pleased her in themselves and because they seemed to signify qualities inextricable from experience. She was most sure that she was
presenting the nature of things not when she could give a clear—
a simplified—explanation but when she could illustrate discontin-
uities. Belief in ultimate oneness was not to deny apparent diversities, what she termed "confusion." Quick statement of other details
of the scene concludes that here the hero, the student, and the
steeple-jack, "each in his way, / is at home." They are at home, we
may assume, because this is a typical human community and these
are types to be found among the "simple people" who live in it.

Yet perhaps these people are not merely simple. The last stanza
opens with the seemingly casual, yet almost heavily ironic remark,
"It could not be dangerous to be living / in a town like this," among
people who have a steeple-jack place danger signs by a church while
he gilds the steeple star that, the poet says, stands for hope. "Simple
people" go about their business; they accept danger and hope as
parts of life. Hope and danger, the poem seems to tell us, are
inextricably mixed in life, are two primary qualities of it. This does
not sadden the poet, for it is a "privilege" to see this mixture, the
multitudinous and often paradoxical combinations of order and dis-
order, calm and storm, faith and doubt that make up our environment; it is exhilarating, her tone tells us. The attitude is that life
is a mixture of possibilities that we would do well to face with an
optimism that may be more than faint though it must be sensibly
restrained.

Cuts from earlier versions eliminated four whole stanzas and portions of two others from the 1951 printing. The longer version
reappears in 1981. The effect of the restored descriptive passages in
this printing is to make the scene itself and the student Ambrose—
mentioned here, though, as noted, also the subject of a now separate
poem—serve as further instances of the paradoxes the poem presents.
The lines detail the scene's mixture of northern and semitropical
flora, the town apparently being one in a northern area warmed by
an ocean current; the passage on the student remarks that he has a
"not-native" hat and books, yet he likes the "elegance" that is native
to the place.

"The Steeple-Jack" was, presumably, the "Part of a Novel" referred to in the original title. In that appearance, the role of "Part
of a Play" was filled by the stanzas titled "The Hero." This title

refers to the ideal citizen of Moore's town, the person who perceives "the rock / crystal thing to see," who retains hope though ground for it has vanished, and who is tolerant of others' errors. The first three stanzas show that the hero is representative; like the rest of us, he has certain dislikes and fears; he vexes some people and is vexed by others. In detailing these aspects of the hero Moore writes with convincing verve: few are so insensitive that they do not shrink when they read that, as any of us might do, the hero shrinks when some unnamed yellow-eyed horror (a bat?) flies out of a hiding place "with quavering water-whistle note, low, / high, in basso-falsetto chirps / until the skin creeps."

As often in her writing, Moore's method here was to set down tersely general statements—that the hero does not like such requirements as "going where one does not wish / to go" and "suffering and not / saying so"—and then to give a vivid exemplification of the appropriate emotion.

Having woven a groundwork of specifics and illustration, Moore in her last three stanzas moves on to commentary that is broader in scope though still conveyed by example and illustration. The hero in his hopefulness and tolerance is lenient toward human error even when its source is plain silliness. An instance is the behavior of a guide at Washington's tomb in Mount Vernon, Virginia, who maintains his decorum and his "reverence for mystery" despite the trivial questioning of a tourist "hobo" who uses her tongue instead of her eyes. The hero thus is true to his own nature. Moses, we are told, "would not be grandson to Pharaoh"; we are to recall that Moses, found and raised by Pharaoh's daughter, upon reaching adulthood left the Egyptians to lead the oppressed Hebrews whom he felt to be his own people. Yet the hero eats what is not his "natural meat": he does, it would seem, not what might give him pleasure but, like Moses, what his circumstances make it ethically necessary for him to do.

The concluding commentary, for which all that goes before has carefully prepared us, is that the hero sees reality. This is not a mere "sight" such as the woman at Washington's tomb was seeking, but "the rock / crystal thing to see." We deduce that this would be reality of experience and situation, including the nature of one's obligations. A second major quality is that the hero "covets" nothing that he has "let go." The hero desires none of the temptations he has dismissed: he has learned, and he confirms in his behavior, what

truth is and what restraint he must show in confronting it. The
nature of our environment as shown in "The Steeple-Jack" and the
ideal of conduct as explained in "The Hero" are related. The hero
recognizes paradox and, seeing it, does not evade it. Like the guide
at the tomb and like Moses in Egypt, he has the self-discipline
necessary under his circumstances. Seeing clearly, he does what he
has to do. Clear sight includes a recognition of ethical responsibility,
a responsibility that is as much a part of reality as mausoleum stone
and desert sand.

The reality that the hero perceives is the topic of the next three
poems. "The Jerboa" has two sections contrasting wasteful and
artificial luxury with spare but genuine simplicity. The opening
lines of "Too Much," the poem's first section, indicate that the
picture the stanzas are to present will be unfavorable. A Roman,
we are told, had his artist "contrive"—a word Moore used to imply
falsity in execution—a fountain of indeterminate shape, somewhat
like a pine cone or a fir cone. Since to Moore precision was of high
value, the point that the shape is imprecise suggests a serious fault.
Looking like something suited for the luxuriant courts of ancient
Egypt, this object has nevertheless passed for art.

The remaining sixteen stanzas of the section describe the waste
and artificiality of the Pharaohs, citing their use of slaves, their
lordly misuse of animals, their coy games. All their decorative art,
the poem says, was delicately wrought or cleverly done—at a "fine
distance" from such realities as drought. Moore made her point by
building up a series of exact details, though in presenting these she
made her attitudes obvious. In stanza 8, for example, she used "toys"
for such supposedly useful adult objects as toilet boxes and the royal
totem. The strongest condemnation is in stanzas 11 and 12, which
remark that dwarfs, kept to lend an "evident"—too obvious—
"poetry" to the court scene, gave it a "fantasy" and a "verisimilitude"
that seem right in any age to "those with . . . power over the
poor." The whole environment was grotesque, a distortion, even a
perversion, of what life should be: the court of the Pharaohs was an
enormous falsity built on the toil of workers who meant no more
to their masters than a fancy cane or a clever folding bedroom. In
pastoral-like court games, princes dressed as women, and women
as men; the Pharaoh "gave his name" to images of serpents and
beetles, and "was named for them"—he was, that is, like these
lifeless parodies of reality.

The last stanzas mention Pharaoh's mongoose, kept to kill the very snakes whose images figured in court rites and games. The pampering of this creature suggests by contrast the naturalness of the jerboa, which had, we may assume, an entirely different and better kind of "happiness." Unlike the mongoose, which was "restless" under the fondling and restraint of its artificial existence, the jerboa had "rest" and "joy" in its desert setting, a home lacking the comforts of court life but providing necessities. "One"—anyone who perceives sensibly—would prefer the jerboa's life to that of the mongoose.

Mention of "plenty" in the last line of the first section leads to the second section, "Abundance." This presents nine stanzas of delighted observation of the jerboa. The speaker gives no overt moralizing, but the exhilaration with which she recounts the details suggests the creature's function as an example of one's living in awareness of himself and his surroundings. His adaptation does not give him a shallow reaction to his circumstances, for he is neither "well adjusted" nor gloomy, neither conservative nor progressive. Like a desert Thoreau, he is in this world to *live* in it.

"Africanus," the section begins, should have meant not the Roman conqueror who was spoken of reverently under that title, but those "untouched" by greed and pride: the freeborn jerboa and the native "blacks" whose harmony with their surroundings is ignored by the supposed great men who are blinded by greed and pride. The man Jacob was led by a mirage to see a ladder to heaven; but the jerboa's perceptions are not mistaken. It can alternately rest and leap, it can hop like a chipmunk or launch itself into the air like a bird as occasion demands; it is "simplified" to efficiency. It is typical of Moore's rigorous though wryly gentle perceptions that she sees the moon not as having sentimentally prettified the jerboa but as having "silvered" it to "steel." The moon and the jerboa both being in harmony with the place, the one strengthens the other.

The theme of harmony is continued through the seventh stanza, where the jerboa is pictured as "assuming" the color of the desert sands; that his paws folded close in to his torso seem of a piece with it rather than attachments to it also suggests a kind of physical wholeness to the creature himself. The last two stanzas make appropriate use of terms and images drawn from music to marvel at the jerboa's way of running; they say that his very footprints are

like impressions of fern seed (a magical substance in Moore's poem
"Spenser's Ireland"). The closing lines suggest setting his leaps to
music, admire the "Chippendale" artistry of his claw, and hint again
at his wholeness by mentioning that his three-toed claw is matched
by his resting posture on two feet and tail.

There is rigor of perception throughout the poem: a tail is a tail,
not a plume or banner; a claw is a claw, not a pedestal. Yet the
effect is not harsh, partly because possible severity is made rich by
the counterpoint of rhythm. In the first section the pace is relatively
slow and careful, as though Moore wants to make sure that the
scorn of her lines is understood. The formal metrics of the second
section is the same as that of the first—there is the same number
of syllables in parallel lines, the same number of lines in stanzas,
the same rhyme scheme. But the section is faster in pace. This
quickening matches in its tripping effects the imagery drawn from
musicianship; and it contributes to the celebratory tone Moore desired for her presentation of the creature that lives not in a surfeit
of artificial "plenty" but in that genuine harmony with his surroundings that to the poet constitutes true "abundance."

The next two poems also ponder the contrast between the merely
luxuriant, the artificial or spurious, and the natural, the genuine,
which, though it may be beautiful, is also useful. "Camellia Sabina"
contrasts the pampered flower of that name and the carefully tended
grape used for wine making with the equally cared for food grape,
and of course says the latter is preferable. Using a relatively long
line, Moore gave the poem a slow pace, a tone that is reflective
though wry. The intention is that we are to take it seriously but
not grimly.

Moore's speaker begins as often with a specific example in mind,
here a camellia sabina she has seen packed in a jar of French plum
brandy. Typically she states the name of the packer and specific
details of the appearance of the jar, and she remarks upon the
similarity in appearance of the flower and the jam. She obviously
delights in the slightly difficult sound clusters of the eighth and
ninth lines, sounds perhaps intended to parallel the somewhat prickly
imagery in the lines: the camellia is a "graft-grown briar-black
bloom," the liquor is "black-thorn pigeon's blood." The description
of the bottle as having "unevenly blown" initials and a green bubble
gives details that in another poem might hint only at a lifelike
imperfection but in this context seem almost to indicate a flaw in

ethics. Perhaps too the choice of such words as "graft" and "foil" is intended to imply the idea of deceit: after remarking that the jar is sealed with foil, the stanza ends with the terse comment "appropriate custom." (A cryptic note in Moore's notebook for 1932–35, dated 4 April 1933, reads: "Camellia sabina. You are accounted tame & domesticated & so may be allowed to do it I suppose if you like." One suspects that this observation had to do with some action in Moore's own life; if it applies in the poem, it may indicate again the idea of appearance being deceptive.)

That such a decorative but useless flower was packaged with what to Moore was misused food is in character. We are next told that "they"—the French—keep camellias under glass for study, and practice other "cruel" customs with useful plants. If the speaker is humorous here, she is also at least partly serious; for she is making artificiality seem, if not quite a sin, at least a grievous error of perception and understanding. In elaborating her description of the camellia, she speaks of its petals as "amanita-white"; the amanita is a poisonous fungus. The third stanza ends with lines detailing the care necessary in some climates to raise camellias, implying that the decorative flower is a fussy one.

The remaining five stanzas present and comment upon the grape and various associations suggested by it. Juxtaposition of these stanzas with those on the camellia is made legitimate, so to speak, by a variety of associations: discussion of both the grape and the flower in the French gardening books that the poem has already made use of; contrast between the "scentless" camellia and the bouquet of grape wines; and the circumstance that certain wines come as red or white, the camellia colors. Moore, no wine-lover, had her speaker comment that the food grape is the "true ground" for celebration. This remark, seemingly an offhand one, is the theme for the rest of the poem.

Thought of grapes as food brings up the mouse, the "Prince of Tails," who might stroll in a vineyard. Moore's notes to the poem inform us that details of her mouse portrait in the next lines were suggested by photographs. The mouse of one picture is addressed for a few lines in the second person as the speaker recites delightedly the jewel-like appearance of grapes placed in his cage, the "Persian" care that has been taken to perfect them and to pluck off the immature. This "jewelry" of sungilded grapes is legitimate; that is, it is not meant to deceive, for example, an imagined Tom Thumb

who, mounted on a mouse, might wish to look at the grapes in
their own reflected light, nor to keep him from dashing around at
will in his miniature circus tent. Such grapes are not meant to dazzle
and confuse but to serve; the poem seems in this climactic stanza
to imply that this makes honest what would otherwise be a dishonest
beauty.

The last stanza gives a final dismissal of the spurious. The wine
cellar "accomplishes nothing"; the "gleaning"—the artful care taken
in tending and harvesting—is "more than the vintage," of more
significance than the end product itself despite showy records of
marvelous vintage years. Parentheses enclose two and a half lines
intended to jog the reader's memory about the fussy care necessary
for the camellia, and the poem ends with a final salute to an Italian
food grape.

The themes of "The Jerboa" and "Camellia Sabina" appear again
in "No Swan So Fine," a short, direct attack, scornful and even
sarcastic in tone, on the contrived and false. The opening lines quote
a *New York Times* item reporting that no water is so still as that in
the dead fountains of Versailles. Similarly, no real swan is so "fine"
as that on a Louis XV candelabrum tree. That "fine" is sarcastic in
intent is evidenced by such details as the description of the swan's
body as "chintz china." The very buttons on the candelabrum tree
are "cockscomb-tinted"; the hodge-podge of decorations also includes dahlias, sea urchins, and, ironically, everlastings; the tree's
branches are made up of "polished sculptured / flowers"—that is,
spurious ones. The poem concludes with the terse sentence "The
king is dead." The reader gathers that a king who valued such a
contrivance was "dead" before his actual death: to value such artifice
is to be spiritually dead. The simplicity of the jerboa demonstrates
the restraint characteristic of heroic behavior; the elaborateness of
the camellia and the china swan exemplifies the rank grossness of
the counterfeit. The hero's vision of "rock crystal" will recognize
restraint and reject the false.

The Genuine and the Imagined

The next three poems present exemplifications of the genuine.
"The Plumet Basilisk," a long poem in four sections, celebrates the
basilisk (*basilicus americanus*) lizard of Central America. To this celebration Moore brings bits of zoological information and oddments

of mythological lore; she gives as usual not only presentation of the thing itself, but also varied samplings of the interpretations man has given it. It is, again, the spirit—the *experience* of the thing— that matters, and it is a compound of the literal and the imagined. She uses neither obvious symbolism, nor much in the way of overt statement; but she provides hints and intimations enough to indicate that the creature stands for the America that the exploitative first settlers failed to find and we of later times have not yet recognized.

The poem opens with a section of three stanzas under the subtitle "In Costa Rica," a label conveying a certain irony in that the scene is indeed a "rich coast," though not for the reasons the conquering Spaniards assumed. The first stanza employs one of Moore's favorite devices: the seemingly casual beginning that leads with a surprising rightness to the subject. Here the movement is from the "green" of blazing driftwood to the colorings of the fire opal and then to the "living firework" of the basilisk. That this lizard is "amphibious" is significant; as a creature of both land and water, he can represent the total of natural resources. The name "basilisk" comes from the Greek for "king of animals," a point referred to in the second stanza where the lizard meets his own kinglike reflection when he jumps into a stream. His launching is described in Keatsian imagery as a process in which he first "faints upon the air"; the implication perhaps is that he leaps less from an act of will than from a kind of natural inclination to merge with his own image. The closing lines of the section that celebrate the lizard's all-round capabilities mix details from the story of El Dorado and from Chinese mythology to indicate a universality of application for the qualities he is meant to represent.

The second section, "The Malay Dragon," and the third, "The Tuatera," continue this universalization and introduce legendry that will be important in the long final section. As we in America have our basilisk, so "they," the Asians, have their Malay dragon; one stanza compares and contrasts the habits of the two. The next stanza describes the Malay dragon as the "true divinity" of his land. He is a "harmless god," who can grasp objects while he is in flight and thus, godlike, is seen "conferring wings" on them. He *is* the "serpent-dove," serpent because of the fable that a lizardlike monster was hatched from a cock's egg by a serpent; yet dove because, as a god, he is a kind of holy spirit. Moore also has in mind the evolutionary theory that birds are of reptilian ancestry, a point further illustrated by the third section's mention of "bird-reptile social life." By the end of the second section the reader is aware that the Malay dragon represents the spirit of his place and is, if not quite a god, at least reminiscent of one. In all this description there is, of course, an implied parallel to the basilisk, a parallel also intimated by the third section that quickly sets down references to various lizards of the world—the tuatera of New Zealand, chameleons, and others— and to carved dragons in Copenhagen which "symbolize . . . security."

Having thus presented the object, the lizard himself together with interpretations of it, Moore was ready to make use of it. Again employing the section title "In Costa Rica," she suggests the basilisk's airy, spiritlike qualities by remarking on his abilities when alarmed to run on the water and to puff himself up to what he hopes is frightening size even though he seems to weigh no more than a shadow on a bit of silk. Lines remarking on the basilisk's serpentine appearance and on his ability to bridge one vine to another are perhaps intended to suggest that he is timeless, the serpent being in some mythologies a symbol of eternity.

The image of a shadow on silk brings up the notion that his barred tail resembles a painting of piano keys; the next several stanzas add to the interplay of factual and mythological allusions a variety of images drawn from musical sounds and instruments. These function as devices for presenting sounds and feelings of the jungle night which could scarcely be communicated literally. The imagery makes the lines as vivid as those that in "The Hero" told what men "shrink" from. This vividness leads to the thought that night in the jungle is itself for man the basilisk of legend, the fearsome monster; but for the basilisk of nature night is the time of most security.

The rhythm quickens as stanza 6 remarks that, when startled, a "scared frog"—apparently the basilisk himself—may leap into the water and, swimming with an "excellent awkwardness" (because he is, after all, an inhabitant of the shore), can enact the role of a creature that can be "interchangeably man and fish." This inter- changeability means the basilisk can move up or down like fingers on a harp—up or down, it would appear, the scale of evolution. Passages detailing this movement use short lines and short stanzas, partly to suggest the darting of a lizard in motion but principally to urge intensity of feeling; for these stanzas give the true climax of the poem, an emotional realization of the creature's significances. On the "tightened wires" of a figurative harp, noises grow and change as they will in the "acoustic shell" of the jungle, yet paradoxically the trees, ranked like harp strings, "veil" the "minute noises" of basilisk and jungle. The trees when seen at night resemble the barred tail of the basilisk, appear "black opal emerald opal emerald," in a "harmony of lizard, jungle, and the invisible."

Perhaps the reader is being told that time, and the world, have aspects accessible only to a sensitivity superior to what mankind can hear or see. Yet the basilisk is not a mere romantic symbol. "No anonymous nightingale sings in a swamp," we are told, and Moore from this point on dismisses musical imagery and returns to the meter of earlier sections of the poem. Not a nightingale but "this," a Central American lizard and all he represents, is the "jewel that the Spaniards failed to see," the life and spirit of America. In the closing stanzas Moore shows him hiding in a lake filled with the precious sacrificial objects that the Spaniards sought but failed to find. Unlike such objects, the basilisk is "alive," despite his "temporary loss" to us. A representative of a spirit in nature and time, he remains a marvelous possibility in a land where exploitation rather than understanding has governed man's relations with nature. Exact definition, apt allusion and vivid feeling have made the plumet basilisk a living embodiment of the spirit of the place. (That Moore, author of a poem entitled "O to Be a Dragon!," would give a lizard or lizardlike creature such a role is not surprising. One may note her report to Bryher, in a letter of 31 August 1921, that when practicing photography she posed "five red fringed gilled newts" in a bowl and "even allowed a stinging fly to settle on me" rather than risk upsetting the tableau.)

Another example of the genuine as found in subtropic America is provided in "The Frigate Pelican," a salute to the Caribbean bird of that name as one who can perceive and act without heeding man's commonplace values and his false romanticizing of nature. As printed in *Complete Poems* the work has five and a half stanzas—just under half of the twelve given in *Selected Poems*. The cutting has considerably improved the poem, for the matter that was dropped elaborated upon the action without adding to it. It is a tribute to Moore's artistic conscience that she could bring herself to eliminate what is, in the context, so fine a line as the opening one of the original twelfth stanza; its polysyllabic words made up of alternately harsh and sibilant sounds perfectly suggest the context: "The reticent lugubrious ragged immense minuet. . . ."

The opening stanza of the *Complete Poems* version describes the bird as "uniting levity with strength"; his levity, it will become apparent, is in his naturalness, his understanding and acceptance of his circumstances. The earlier version contrasted him with a carnival-clad human figure; omitting this contrast enables the poem to deal more directly with the bird. The poem's mixture of fairy tale and fact gives it a suitable levity without destroying its strength of assertion.

Recounting various names applied to the bird, Moore speculates at one point that perhaps "swift" is the proper word for him. The reference is to his speed and to the vagaries of popular ornithology, but it may also imply a comparison of him to the lizard ("swift" is the popular term for one variety of lizard). After presenting his gracefulness, the almost ceremonious ease of the whole frigate pelican flock in its hovering flight, and the harmony with nature in which the flock allows the wind to reverse its direction, Moore herself reverses direction in the third stanza a bit, to remark that these birds are not like the swan that is sometimes, in fairy tales, a servant to man. This comment in turn brings on a statement of typical commonplace "mottoes" of that "less limber animal," man— "Make hay; keep / the shop; I have one sheep." The juxtaposition without transition is typical of Moore's style; it is so handled that it leads not to mere intricacy but to suddenness of revelation. This bird, the frigate pelican, would "not know Gretel from Hansel": he is no slave to the perceptions of deluded man. Like Handel, he "hides" in his "art."

Having remarked upon his "strength," and upon his independence from human ideas and his clever "vigilance," Moore now turns to his "levity." She first quotes the Italian motto that one should be gay civilly and then inquires why this should be advised; her reply is a Hindu saying implying that whether one is blessed or cursed depends not on what others think of one but on whether what one does is good or evil. The bird, that is, is not required to be "civil" in the sense of accepting the judgments of others, for he knows that what counts is what he does. He earns his gaiety by right action. The poem closes with lines presenting an extension of this idea. Men romanticize the moon, for example, whereas this "most romantic" bird sleeps in a swamp hidden from moonlight. But he not only avoids what the poem implies is the merely conventional; he also shows an ability that is to be envied: when crushing danger is near, he wakes from his sleep and escapes it. Thus the frigate pelican stands for what in the context of this poem is to be taken as a true romanticism, an independence of mind and an understanding of nature that are superior to the acceptances and sentimentalizations deluding man.

Though independence from man's notions is admirable, service to him in his workaday world may be honorable. "The Buffalo" opens with speculations on possible symbolisms of the black tones of a bison the poet has seen pictured (three lines omitted from the second stanza of early versions made the point that the subject is a print). In the next stanzas Moore reflects upon the evolution from the extinct aurochs to the present-day cow, a development that is something of a descent in biology and, we gather, in value. However, she continues, if we are to consider "human notions," perhaps the "best" creature of the *Bos* genus is the Indian buffalo, a hardworking but independent and spirited animal who is neither customarily bespangled with jewelry like a temple elephant, placidly subservient like a Vermont ox, nor freakish like a painter's imagined animal; he is mettlesome, "free," cheerful, yet capable of fighting off a tiger. His qualities, indeed, are such that he need not feel inferior to "any / of ox ancestry" whether these be the twins of mythology, the aurochs, or the prairie bison. He combines, that is, the virtues of the wild ancestors and of his domesticated contemporaries with those of the oxen of myth. Thus uniting the mundane and the imagined, he is of high value.

"The Buffalo" originally appeared in a magazine together with another poem suggested by a picture, "Nine Nectarines" (originally "Nine Nectarines and Other Porcelain"). In "Nine Nectarines" we see that the poet interested in presenting realities may find the imagined superior to the realistic. The poem contrasts a garden book's poor reproduction of a decorated Chinese plate with a good enameled porcelain picture of a unicorn. The plate is adorned with a painting of nectarines on a twig. The opening stanzas establish the similarity of the nectarines to the peach, which in China symbolized and, indeed, was believed literally to afford, long life. But these nectarines, carelessly depicted by the "unenquiring brush" of the commercial publisher in whose "bookbinding" Moore saw the picture, are on a "much mended" plate—not one blessed with long life—and are reproduced as so unnaturally flawless that one seeing them might doubt that the nectarine was ever a "wild spontaneous" fruit. Moore deftly and somewhat wryly suggests that the garden-book writer supports such doubts by mentioning that he prudently "would not say" whether or not the nectarine was ever domesticated. The demonstration of the inaccuracies possible under the aegis of realism is reinforced by describing the animal also painted on the plate, an animal apparently supposed to represent a real-life creature but one so poorly drawn that it is impossible to tell whether the artist had in mind a moose, horse, or ass.

At this point in the middle of the fourth stanza, later printings drop three and a half stanzas from the *Selected Poems* version. The omitted passages elaborated finely upon the plate's decorations and drew an extra contrast between the rather heavy realism of hunting and domestic scenes in European dinnerware and the perfection of Chinese decorators' control of imagined subjects. The material did not advance the movement of the poem, though we may regret losing such a fine passage as the lines descriptive of a bat in moon-light whose eyes "are separate from the face—mere / delicately drawn gray discs, out from / itself in space."

The conclusion in the cut version of the poem, which comes almost abruptly, remarks that the artistry of the enameled kylin demonstrates that the Chinese race is one which " 'understands / the spirit of the wilderness.' " The ending lines assert that only a "Chinese" imagination, one open to the spirit as well as to the merely literal, could have produced such a masterpiece. Evidence that Moore herself sought to be faithful to the spirit of the object is the fact that the kylin described in this stanza scarcely conforms in detail to the creature described in her notes to the poem. The nectarine and the kylin had special appeal to Moore as subject matter, for the fruit in its kinship to the peach and the mythical animal in its embodiment of male and female could both represent unity. And she sometimes, as in "The Buffalo," sought subjects that can be made to symbolize unity of matter and spirit. That both nectarine and kylin symbolize long life also made comparison of them possible. Since the examples of these subjects she happened on were not of equal artistic merit, she had opportunity for the pointed contrast that is the basis of this poem.

Praise of one who sees reality, declares it directly, and, deservedly proud, defends himself well is the theme of "To a Prize Bird" (originally "To Bernard Shaw: A Prize Bird"). The poem, first published in 1915, was not included in the 1951 collection but reappeared in 1981. That a proper concept of reality will shape proper behavior is also indicated in the next three poems. "The Fish" celebrates courageous independence; "In This Age of Hard Trying, Nonchalance Is Good and" recommends intelligent restraint; and "To Statecraft Embalmed" argues that life must be served even if doing so violates decorum. "The Fish," one of Moore's most celebrated poems, follows one of her typical patterns of organization. It begins with notation of exact details that surround the object; after a sufficient accumulation of these, it moves to a statement of what they indicate about its nature; finally it gives the ethical significance of its qualities. Though this pattern is simpler than the structures of some of her later work, it is not in broad outline essentially different.

In "The Fish" the chief object is a cliff at the ocean shore. The poem, however, begins not with a description of the cliff itself but with a mention of the fish that move about it. That they "wade," rather than swim easily, perhaps indicates that the very water at the base of the defiant cliff takes from it an aura of resistance. The world in which the fish move is dark; there is a suitable parallel between their presence in the steely water and the existence of a spirit within the cliff itself. The "ash-heaps" of mussel-shells, crow-blue in color, include one shell that opens and shuts itself like an "injured fan," a comparison that gives a vividly accurate picture of such a shell's movements and also suggests the peril and hardship of this stern world. There is no refuge of any sort; the very barnacles "cannot hide," for reflected rays from the sun penetrate the crevices in the rock-torn waters and in the cliff itself, almost as though someone were deliberately aiming a spotlight into the cruel turquoise sea. The water has like a chisel "driven" (not eroded or worn) a chasm into the iron of the cliff itself; there ocean creatures are tumbled one over the other. The colors, the textures, the action of sun and water all suggest mortal danger, implacable if impersonal hardness.

In this appropriate setting the cliff looms scarred by "All / external / marks of abuse . . . " from wave and weather. It bears the marks of human assault from the land too, for its face shows "dynamite grooves" and "hatchet strokes." The "chasm-side"—the face the cliff presents to the water, or perhaps the face of the rent that the waves have driven into the rock—is "dead." Yet, abused though it is, the cliff paradoxically can "live on," can feed its spirit on the harshness that ages it. The assaulting sea, not the resistant cliff, wearies under the strain of the perpetual battle.

For Moore the cliff seems to represent an ideal. Battered by that sea which—as in "A Grave" and "The Steeple-Jack"—symbolizes the peril of existence, the cliff demonstrates the capacity of the courageous in spirit to triumph. Like William Faulkner's mankind, it does not merely survive but will prevail. Later versions use a five-line stanza that gives an effect of relatively greater thoughtfulness than the faster-paced six-line stanza of earlier printings.

Though Moore greatly admired the bold endurance that may be wounded but is never worn away, she saw that another kind of value may be necessary in human circumstances. How an artist might proceed is the subject of "In This Age of Hard Trying, Nonchalance Is Good and." This work is one of the few early poems in which Moore does not have in mind a well-defined "object"—animal, work of art, scene—to provide her with analogies, allusions, or other sources for the leap of interpretation that brings her to her poem. In this poem the dependence is on an implied story. The situation apparently arises from her speculation upon the quotation from Dostoyevski that opens the poem, " 'really, it is not the / business of the gods to bake clay pots' " (she has added the conversational "really" to the quotation). "They," the gods, would not bake pots on one occasion, she tells us; some of them enwrapped themselves in their own egos as though thinking contemptuously that communion with others, "excessive popularity," would be a mere "pot," a worthless goal. The result was that an ability that might have "split the firmament" had no effect. Discarding itself, this power fell on "some poor fool" and gave him a talent for storytelling. His tales were not realistic but, being inspired, were far better than the dull "certitude" of routine talkers.

Perhaps he was something of a reformer in ethics; proceeding by indirection, possibly by such semi-fables as Moore herself was fond of, he was more effective in his "by-play" than were the direct sermonizings of the uninspired. His restraint, therefore, is the best means to the "self-protectiveness" that is a true weapon because, we gather, it enables accomplishment that the self-centered behavior of the gods in this story could not achieve. They cut themselves off from others, but desirable self-restraint would result in freedom of perception and truth of expression, not in isolation. The best garb or pose for the self-protective is that of the wanderer who has no alliances that might unnerve him for the campaign he must wage. The long title of the poem, making up the first half of a sentence that is completed in the first two lines of the poem, taken together with the ending, suggests the recommendation that in this age of competitive and obvious effort, an artful casualness is the best manner for the poet.

Yet "nonchalance" in attitude is not to mean evasion of responsibilities, a point demonstrated by "To Statecraft Embalmed," which scolds whoever would recommend discretion as better policy than justice. The poem is an address to the sacred ibis of ancient Egypt. The ibis was often identified with Thoth, the moon-god who in some aspects was regarded as the agent of creation-by-words, the founder of the arts and sciences, and hence the source of wisdom and magic. Mummified remains of the ibis were often therefore placed in the tombs of Egyptian rulers along with secret inscriptions intended to guide and magically protect the dead.

The title, we may note uses "statecraft," not "statesmanship." The bird-god addressed is apparently mummified, for, under "hard" plumage, he is guarding a secret in a sarcophagus. He is told that there is "nothing to be said for" him, and he is sarcastically advised to conceal his secret. The fourth line consists of only the single-letter word "O," and each fourth line thereafter is a monosyllable rhyming with it: the effect is that of a mocking litany, ironically aping the reverent words addressed to such a bird in ancient Egypt. The bird is a "necromancer," one gifted with the power to talk with the dead and, in the poem, with the power to speak from the tomb. As the god of wisdom, he is asked whether the idea of Justice, perhaps as inscribed or symbolized in the tomb, should be allowed to come to life. Leaving the tomb to respond, the bird-god says no; and he magically winds about "us," his questioners, a "snow" of silence which he deepens with "moribund" talk. What he recommends, it appears, is the "discretion" that statesmen often value above right action.

The poem now editorializes, declaring that such crafty behavior is not in our day "statesmanlike." The bird-god protests that giving embodiment to an ancient "grace" is more important than justice, but the poem replies that life, despite its flaws, is better than decorum: justice is a live quality; decorum may be a dead one. The last nine lines angrily predict that one so out of touch with necessities will fail to see the unreality of his actions; his "suicidal" dreams, perhaps of power and national glory, will drive him to attack his friends and fatally to embrace his foes. This is one of Moore's few poems on political ethics. Even in it, of course, the political element is only a vehicle for conveying the point that in any circumstances justice is to be valued more than discretion; life, more than social propriety.

Poetry and the Poet

It is a truism that all poems are "about" poetry. At least the next nine pieces in *Complete Poems* are more or less direct treatments of poetry itself and of the poet and his critics. In "Poetry" Moore stated something of her own artistic creed; in "Pedantic Literalist," "Critics and Connoisseurs," and "The Monkeys," she commented upon criticism; in "In the Days of Prismatic Color," "Peter," "Picking and Choosing," "England," and "When I Buy Pictures," she presented particular aspects of her aesthetics.

In its complete form "Poetry" contains Moore's most comprehensive reflections on her art. Since she customarily made decisions for artistic reasons, it is most likely that she became dissatisfied with the poem's views or with the way it expresses them. It is also possible that she was tired of the endless rehashing of the poem by critics. Whatever her motive, in her last revision she retained only two and a half of the first three lines of the 1951 version. The resulting fragment amounts to an abstract summary of her position, lacking the detail that made the position vividly comprehensible. The editors of the 1981 collection complied with her wishes by publishing the abbreviated version in the text; fortunately, in the view of most readers, they gave the full version in the notes. I will discuss this version. The beginning assertion that "I, too, dislike it" is sometimes quoted as evidence that Moore was a good sophisticate who did not take her art seriously, that under the skin she was essentially a middle-class intellectual without unmodish convictions. But to so read her is to read quite wrongly. Though the remark is on the face of it ironic, it is more than a simple comment of obvious indirection. She was declaring her disgust with the common view of poetry as a way of prettifying standard opinions, usually those of intellectual liberalism. The critics who read her as having contempt for all poetry are thus hoisted on their own petard: the kind of poetry she disliked is, or includes, that which they commonly prefer. What she liked is "the genuine"; the rest of "Poetry" is an effort at explanation of this quality.

Her speaker declares, in lines reminiscent of T.S. Eliot's "The Hollow Men," that vivid presentation of the specific details of a subject is important not because it may lead to "high-sounding interpretation" but because it is "useful": because it can lead to the "genuine." But if these details are only "derivative," removed from the actuality of the experience, none of us will admire them. The "us" is delightfully and pointedly represented as creatures engaged in a variety of activities; the passage deftly scores the "immovable critic" as a horse to whom the work of art is a flea. No one, the poem is saying, is likely to be diverted from his usual concerns by anything other than the accurately presented. All the "us" are possible subjects; even the business and schoolroom documents sometimes excluded from the canon of literary material may be used for poetry.

Yet, as these inclusions would indicate, the mere thing in itself is not a poem: "half poets" who celebrate the humdrum detail for its own sake do not thereby make poetry. What is important is that the poet be true ultimately, not to fact but to his imagination; poets must be "literalists of the imagination," above the insolence of expecting presentation of the trivial to be poetry. The poet must give " 'imaginary gardens with real toads in them' "—a populace of real objects that, taken together, will produce an imagined experience. Perhaps no one at present has achieved such art; meanwhile, one may qualify as being "interested in poetry" if he demands fulfillment of the objectivist paradox that "rawness," the accurate presentation of the thing itself, must be the basis for, the material of, a "genuine" garden that is more than the sum of its physical components.

This theory is, of course, ultimately a neoromantic one; for it requires something more than realism of observation. It does insist, however, that one start from the accurately realized object. In Moore's creed, poetry must climb to heights beyond realism, but it must begin its ascent on a stairway of fact. The enameled kylin of "Nine

Nectarines" was a better object of art than the painted fruit, though
delineated with perhaps equal inaccuracy because his creator perceived the spirit within him.

In rhetorical form "Poetry" follows one of Moore's common patterns; moving from an artfully casual beginning to a climax of feeling
in the next-to-last stanza, it then ends almost off-handedly with a
final, fairly direct comment upon what has been presented. As a
work of art, it is its own exemplification. Though it deals more
directly with an abstract subject than most of her work, it is grounded
on a sufficient quota of such specificities as "hair that can rise," a
bat upside down, a "wild horse taking a roll." Because it is provided
with these concrete details, it is much more successful than "In This
Age of Hard Trying, Nonchalance . . . ," in which the subject is
equally abstract but the incident the poem is based upon is not
clearly delineated.

Each of the remaining eight poems on poetry works through a
particular object or set of circumstances. The injunction in "Poetry"
that one must be a "literalist of the imagination" does not, of course,
mean approval of the "Pedantic Literalist" who is disparaged in the
poem of this title. The chief error of the mundanely minded is
illustrated as deceptiveness: his failure to perform what he seems to
promise. Such a literalist is termed in the opening line a "Prince
Rupert's drop" (a blob of glass so treated that it appears attractive
but flies apart when handled) and a "paper muslin ghost," a spurious
spirit that would crumple if embraced. A further comparison is to
a heart that, failing to give warning of its weakness, caused its
owner's death. The result of long practice at deception—perhaps
of trying vainly and unimaginatively to make poetry out of the
merely literal—is that the spontaneity with which even the "literalist" is born turns into wood.

The "hardihood" that resists spontaneities is the topic of "Critics
and Connoisseurs," a poem opening with the somewhat resounding
remark that there is "a great amount of poetry in unconscious/
fastidiousness." Certain "products" of conscious fastidiousness are
"well enough in their way," the poem continues, but such spontaneous attempts at careful procedure as a child's efforts to right a
toy and to feed a puppy are better acts of art because they are
unforced. Another example of overdone fastidiousness is a swan
remembered as reluctant to give up its "disbelief," its false dignity,
in order to eat food thrown to it. In the third stanza the poem turns

to "you," the critics and connoisseurs who, like the swan, have "ambition without understanding." An illustration of the fault is furnished by the behavior of an ant that foolishly continued attempts to find a use for burdens that could contribute nothing to ant goals. The poem ends with an inquiry: of what use are such ambitions as those of the swan and the ant, ambitions to maintain an impenetrable reserve or to demonstrate that one has struggled for a useless trophy? Remembering the comment in "Poetry" that objects are good if in some sense useful, we may deduce that critics, like the swan, and connoisseurs, like the ant, are guilty of adopting attitudes and of choosing goals that could be valuable if intended to serve some useful purpose but are often clung to without understanding. The poem is recommending more attention to the spirit, less to the letter.

"The Monkeys" makes it clear that, though the artist is to find a "spirit" in the object, his enterprise is not to be an expedition into the "arcanic." The poem, which begins with comments upon sights observed during a long-past trip to a menagerie (or a parliament of literary critics?) remarks on the difficulty of recalling in detail the reasons for the impression of "magnificence" that remains. But one creature will not be forgotten, a large, kingly cat who perhaps represents those described at the end of "Poetry" as "interested in poetry." He, it seems, gave the indignant speech of the last two stanzas of "The Monkeys," a protest against critics' imposition of "inarticulate frenzy" and their insistence on almost "malignant" depths in poetry. Moore, an impressionist in her own criticism, was again arguing for the spontaneous rather than the codified and pseudo-profound that she apparently believed typical of the "immovable" critic of "Poetry," the "consciously fastidious" interpreter of "Critics and Connoisseurs."

The ease with which she had a cat deliver a comment, almost a diatribe, on literary criticism demonstrates the art in the seemingly casual beginning and an ending that give a rightness to the choice of a feline spokesman. Having an animal convey the message provides a neat irony; the poem's original title, "My Apish Cousins," made somewhat more obvious the ironic comparison of human and animal.

(The unimaginative literalist was again a target in "Melanchthon," a work printed in 1951 but omitted from the 1981 book. It closes with a question that amounts to an assertion of the belief that the depth of a life and of a poet's work will not be perceived by one who fails to sense the "unreason" or mystery that Moore believed to lie behind all experience.)

Yet though the poet is not be "consciously fastidious" and is to see an "unreason," he is nevertheless to be clear. "In the Days of Prismatic Colour" declares that early in creation color was "fine" or exact, not because of art but because of its closeness to its origins. Even "obliqueness," indirection, was apparent and understandable, not hidden. But now the oblique is no longer accessible, and color no longer holds its purity; original simplicity has been replaced by "complexity." Though there is nothing wrong with complexity when it reflects actual perception, it is wrong when indulged in to the point that it obscures. And it is especially wrong when made an end in itself, when a poet values the vehemence instead of the worth of what he is saying, and insists that all truth must be dark. Such insistence, being "principally throat," is a "sophistication" that is the direct opposite to truth.

Sophisticates, it appears, view the truth as something like a monster of Greek myth, crawling, gurgling, and darksome. "To what purpose!," she exclaims, are the perverse misunderstandings that see truth as complex and even as monstrous. Truth is "no Apollo / Belvedere, no formal thing": it is, we gather, spontaneous and unconscious. Though complexity may appear in it, not this but courage and endurance are its chief characteristics. The "wave" of critical fashion, of philosophical challenge, may roll over it; but, like the cliff in "The Fish," it will survive.

The virtue of being "natural," of doing without pretense or alibi what one is designed to do, is celebrated with appropriate playfulness in "Peter," a presentation of a cat belonging to two of Moore's women friends and a demonstration of her ability to exemplify in a poem the virtues she was meditating upon in the process of writing it. The observations of Peter that she sets down are those identified with what might be called his cat-ness: complete relaxation, narrowed eyes, obvious nightmares, and lack of concern with judgment that would condemn him for possessing the claws and tail he was born with. Emphasis is upon his animality, his unself-conscious turning from the coddled to the clawing and back again. The poem has been read as an attack on Catholicism, the cat representing the church that claims to have been founded by the apostle Peter and that to some Protestants has appeared as both lethargic and rapacious. The poem has even been read as a feminist attack on Catholicism's failure to ordain women. But it takes a considerable stretch to read into the piece an attack on another Christian church: the focus is on the cat in his cat-ness, not on use of him as a symbol, and when the poem appeared in 1924 neither Moore's own Presbyterian church nor other mainline denominations were ordaining women. Remaining unabashed by the "published fact"—his obvious animality—and willing "to purloin, to pursue" as instinct bids him, Peter the cat is a living example of natural behavior.

That naturalness is essential for the literary critic, who should see literature as "a phase of life," is the assertion of "Picking and Choosing." The advice is, as in "In the Days of Prismatic Colour," that we should not approach literature with fearful reverence. And, as in the passage in "Poetry" dismissing "half poets," we must not come to it as though it were merely commonplace. In his statement the critic must use the "true" word, avoiding the murky and the faked. As examples of the kind of "fact" that critics should give, the speaker presents capsule comments on Shaw and Henry James that mention flaws in their work but also point to virtues. (The comment on James has changed several times. The first version said flatly that James "is not profound"; later versions say that James is all that he is said to be "if feeling is profound"; the 1981 book reads "James / is all that has been said of him".)

Moore concludes the passage with lines observing that Thomas Hardy, for example, should be seen not primarily as either novelist or poet but as a writer conforming to a dictum like T. S. Eliot's assertion that one should interpret life through "the medium of the emotions." "The Monkeys" shows Moore's own preference for criticism that has an emotional basis and her scorn for merely intellectual methods. She did in "Picking and Choosing" concede that, if the critic must have an opinion, he may be permitted to "know what he likes." The next lines admit Gordon Craig and Kenneth Burke to the rank of good critic, both apparently having impressed Moore as knowing what they like.

Thought of Burke brings up the phrase *summa diligentia*, which Moore translated (in the essay "Humility, Concentration, and Gusto") as "with all speed." These words remind the speaker of the schoolboy mistranslation of the Latin as meaning "on top of the diligence," an example of one kind of bad literary criticism. In a tone of reasonableness the poem then comments that "We are not daft about the meaning" but that the "familiarity" critics exhibit with "wrong meanings" is puzzling. The next several lines address those who exhibit such familiarity, adjuring them that, for example, the simple candle should not be seen as an electrified mechanism. The last six lines ostensibly are addressed to a dog yapping to the world at large his daydream that he has caught a badger. He is told that he should remember that, even if he had really accomplished the feat, he would scarcely need to make such a clamor about it. The moral is that the critic should give hints, a few spontaneous reactions, not mystification and not boasts of imagined retrievals. The poet is recommending the process named in her title: the "picking and choosing" that she considered to be primarily a task for the emotions, not for powers of abstraction and analysis. We may note that Moore could be reasonably impersonal in her opinions of critics, for her work had been praised since the 1920s by Yvor Winters, R. P. Blackmur, Kenneth Burke, Eliot, Stevens, and Williams—a range including "new critics," impressionists, and eclectics.

Appearances and Realities

A certain naturalness—lack of apparent artifice—is the quality Moore defended in America, the country that the poem somewhat paradoxically entitled "England" is principally about. Its opening stanzas cite various examples of neatness of finish or of civilized proficiency in Europe and Asia; without transition, the poem then begins to detail characteristics observed in America, a list not of abstract qualities but of such specifics as the smoking of cigars on the street. The tone of the passage has a playfulness indicative of Moore's affection for the homey detail she is listing. The poem turns serious, however, as allusion to different ways of pronouncing English brings up the assertion that such a matter should not give rise to "continents of misapprehension." The consequent reflection follows that not every mushroom that appears to be poisonous is really unsafe, a metaphor implying that not every American trait is to be condemned without reflection. A listing, so rapidly paced as to seem to tumble out, of great qualities in European and Asian civilizations ends with an approving allusion to the practical wisdom of Izaak Walton. That a person may not have met greatness in America is not proof that it does not exist: it has never been "confined to one locality." The surface of homely fact in America may be deceiving to the Europophile who identifies greatness with conscious fastidiousness, so to speak. The poem's success is due partly to its vivid particularization of national qualities. The novel use of colons in the first and second stanzas, perhaps intended to imply that one detail is strengthened by the next, is also found in the poem "The Labors of Hercules."

To fail to see possibilities in America is to err in perception—to trust in stereotypes instead of in spontaneity of observation. More serious is failure to see what in Moore's opinion are spiritual forces that lie within all the world of appearances. She asserts the point overtly in "When I Buy Pictures." This poem lists subjects for painting that would give the speaker, surely Moore herself, "pleasure in my average moments." The examples are pictures that would be notable for "intensity of mood" or for charm of content. The passage leads to a dismissal of "Too stern an intellectual emphasis." Further qualifications are that the pleasing must not be an attempt "to disarm," to argue or deceive; and it must not be one of those paintings commonly accepted as masterpieces only because others have not had equal publicity. Whatever the desirable picture may deal with, it must convey emotional insight: it must "acknowledge the spiritual forces which have made it." The somewhat longer, earlier version of this piece was more obviously insistent on the necessity that a picture arouse an individualistic response in each observer and be the product of a particular artist; perhaps Moore felt this early version to be too editorial.

Thus the poet is qualified as one of the "literalists of the imagination," for he will maintain a spontaneity of reaction and impression; he will reject stereotypes and ponderous systems in order to be open to understanding that can come to him only by faiths and intimations. He is not to show sensory reality only because that reality has value in itself, but because, in showing it accurately, he will discover the "spiritual" that informs it. The spirit, that is, is not a mystery; it is as much a part of reality as the material.

Belief in the existence of a spiritual world did not mean that Moore was content with received optimisms. The fact that courage was her principal value, that she thought the advisable existence to be an armored one, indicated that her world was one wherein danger always threatens. In "The Steeple-Jack" and in "The Fish" the sea was a challenge and threat, a symbol of forces to be resisted with

bravery and independence. The ever-present perils of existence are
the subject of her poem on the sea, significantly entitled "A Grave."
In it the sea is beautiful, tempting, and challenging. But it concedes
nothing; it is totally inhuman; and, more than impersonal, it is
malign. The poem opens as an address to a man who is apparently
blocking others' view in order to look at the ocean himself;[2] his
rudeness is an example of the greed that governs men's attitudes.
The poem warns him he can expect nothing from the sea but "a
well excavated grave." Man's day-to-day environment, represented
by a stand of firs, gives no hint of any feelings; but the sea is not
a practitioner of such "repression": it returns quickly any "rapacious"
looks that are given it. The poem recounts warningly the fate of
men who lost their lives in attempting to conquer the sea. On the
water's surface cautious men go about their business of netting for
fish, not aware that they are "desecrating a grave," acting as though
there were no death, yet perhaps betraying a recognition as they
row quickly away.

We are not told of any happening, but from the sixteenth line
the mood changes. The rest of the poem seems an astringently
pitying account of how the ocean, though having perhaps just
drowned a man, continues in its age-old, beautiful indifference. The
waves move on, the birds and the bell-buoys call, and the ocean
deceptively looks as though it were not that sea in which "dropped
things" die so quickly that any movement they perform is caused
only by its waters. The dangers hinted at in "The Steeple-Jack"
have occurred; yet the sea remains as treacherously attractive as ever.
The implied moral is not that one should be fearful but that he
should be cautious: courage is not foolhardiness. The perils of existence are perhaps not always apparent; but, like spiritual forces,
they are real and must be recognized. The reader may be reminded
of Williams's poem "The Yachts," which has similarities in idea
and execution.

There are, of course, less fatal perils for man. Undue sophistication
is the topic of two poems. In "Those Various Scalpels" Moore presents a woman dressed in high fashion, brilliant but artificial. Having in mind such poems as "No Swan So Fine" and "In the Days
of Prismatic Colour," the reader is scarcely surprised to find that
aspects of the woman's appearance are compared to stone and ice;
indeed, the details are so ludicrously exaggerated that one is reminded of Shakespeare's sonnet spoofing "false compare." The wom-

an's appurtenances, designed to rustle "conventional opinion," are "rich instruments" with which to study or experiment with life. But, asks the poet, why do this with instruments more sophisticated than life itself? Life, that is, is relatively simple and frank; understanding of it is open to all who, like the cat in "Peter," are willing to respond naturally.

Sophisticates of various sorts are targets of the series of sarcasms in "The Labors of Hercules." They include such mistaken people as those "of austere taste" who refuse to recognize that creativity demands freedom and as those of "fourteen carat ignorance" who pose as sages. There are, the poem concludes, certain fixed values; for example, "one keeps on knowing" that members of other religions or nationalities are decent people—a moral principle Moore would reassert in the poem "In Distrust of Merits." "The Labors of Hercules" is essentially a series of citations of errors in attitude or feeling, and each is contrasted scornfully with what Moore felt to be a genuine principle.

The sophisticate sees himself as a member of his society's elite, as one especially aware of fashionable refinements in behavior. Two poems deal particularly with the importance of one's social environment. The first of these, "New York," declares that it is not the "plunder" that makes city life important, but the "accessibility to experience" that it affords. She selects one aspect of the variety that is New York, its function as the center of the wholesale fur trade. This is useful synechdoche, enabling her in small space to obtain a coherent variety of imagery and metaphor; and it is something more than a merely coy conceit, for furs are obtained at some cost in animal pain and human effort, and function as one of the principal status symbols in our society.

Yet the fur business is not the real city, the one that matters to an aware human being. Indeed, the glamor and hustle of the fur trade, of commercial life generally, are a "savage's romance," "a dime-novel exterior." What matters about an environment is not the material powers and advantages it may afford, but the variety of opportunity it offers for some degree of "experience." Allusions to the fur trade of frontier days and descriptions of the modern city in terms drawn from that trade make for a humor that helps avoid didacticism, and they also suggest an ironic view of New York's boasted status as a cultural center: here, indeed, in the artificial "ingenuity" of commerce is the reason for the city's being.

From consideration of her city she moves to more general reflections in "People's Surroundings." This poem explores the paradox, stated in the opening lines of its final stanza, that men develop behaviors intended to put an artful surface on motivations they may not wish to have exposed; yet, if we see accurately, we discover that appearances are not concealments but rather a guide to the nature of a man. What he does, where he lives, how he builds and furnishes—these are a surface "exterior" to his central self. Yet this exterior is intimately linked with the self and is indicative of its nature. The poem opens with four short stanzas presenting types of surroundings in which people may be found, from a simple room to a palace, a modern business building, and a wealthy estate. Though the statement of these settings indicates approval of the simple and delight in the colorful, and shows rejection of the sophisticated and the sterile, it functions principally as a demonstration of the variety in human circumstances. The fifth and sixth stanzas present the mind that "moves in a straight line"—the frank, direct mind of Utah or Texas that, despite apparent simplicity, raises perhaps as many questions as it answers. There is also the self-conscious mind whose typical product is the tropical elegance of Bluebeard's Tower with its cruel history, lush gardens and furnishings, memories of fragile ladies, and encouragement of excessive self-analyses. In all these circumstances it is apparent that men's guiding desire has been for a kind of concealment.

The poem ends not with a rhetorical conclusion but with six lines listing roles in human life and another six listing places where these are typically carried out. Despite attempts at concealment, the "exterior and the fundamental structure" are one: captains and cooks are indeed found in camps and dining halls. Moore believed in the existence of a spiritual realm, but did not deny or denigrate realism. She sought to work through it and, indeed, found that only by means of accurate portrayal could she successfully hint at or discover whatever may lie behind appearances.

Appearances may, of course, be puzzling. "Snakes, Mongooses, Snake-Charmers and the Like" records musings occasioned by a friend's interest in exotic animals from India and particularly in an asp possessed by a snake charmer. The friend used to be interested in humble animals; but now all his admiration is focused on the asp, at which he gazes as though he were charmed. As the asp stands in its basket, its perfection of shape and its rhythm make even one who dislikes it feel "compelled" to look at it. Speculating about the possible meaning of such a creature, the poem mentions the importance the snake has had in human cultures since antiquity. Conceding that it is as "fine" as its worshipers have held it to be, the poem nevertheless suggests that perhaps the snake was invented to demonstrate or to remind us that when "intelligence in its pure form" has found an endeavor to be "unproductive," it "will come back." Perhaps the intimation is that the snake is a reminder of the Garden of Eden, a sign of guilt that has been left to warn that, if man turns out in the long run to be an "unproductive" development in the universe, intelligence may erase him and start creation over again. The question can't be answered; all that we can be sure of is the snake's perfection of form. There is no point in protesting the friend's fascination or the existence of the snake. Attempts to correct people or circumstances that we do not understand often spring from pride; the best policy is to allow free expression to a "distaste" that, being natural, is not prideful.

Two satires on types of writers also deal with the relationship between appearances and reality. "Bowls," which reports pleasure in the sight of lawn bowling, compares it with the meticulous art of Chinese lacquer carving and says that survival of a game with so much punctilio enjoins us in our day to be "precisionists" rather than hasty "Pompeians" whose panic is as permanent as the lavas of Vesuvius, though our letter-writing would suggest us to be panicked indeed. The intention is obviously sarcastic; it may also be ironic, for we cannot help remembering that in bowling the pattern of pins is suddenly disrupted. The impression of irony is reinforced as we read that the speaker of the poem, having reluctantly decided that as precisionists her contemporaries are worth some attention, reports her resolve to answer the questions she receives in the mail from them. But the questions now solemnly cited (why do you like winter better than summer?) are evidence that the correspondents are indeed hasty priers for the trivial. The speaker will answer quickly, for in so doing she "gives twice."

"Novices" is an attack on fashionable litterateurs who proclaim themselves to be the "good and alive young men." They do not think it necessary for writers to be familiar with their subject matter; they engage in excessive and pompous analyses of deliberately abstruse work and hold themselves superior to writers who draw on simple sources. Such novices are, in a word, sophisticates. Heedless of the matters of diction, tone, and substance which should interest them, they indulge in inanity and in vapid praises of writers they do not understand. The poem closes with a passage that sets down the ocean-like virtues of Hebrew, a language Moore cites as one example of the kind of knowledge needful for a writer that novices refuse to acquire. The poem is notable for its imaginative, specific presentation of the faults it is condemning and of the contrasting virtues of the Hebrew that represents any "spontaneous unforced passion" that is genuine.

One of several qualities novices lack is the discipline that not only is an important value in Moore's ethics but also is frequently her subject for a poem. The paradox that liberty may be bred by self-discipline, a restraint in action and expression, is explored in the long poem "Marriage." The tone is somewhat humorous, sympathetic yet at times mockingly ironic; the strategy, unusual for Moore but appropriate in this poem, includes a report of an imagined dialogue between an Adam and Eve who are not so much the characters of the Garden of Eden as representatives of married woman and man. The lines are fairly short, usually six to eight syllables; lines of twelve or more syllables are usually followed by lines of four or five. The tone, the mixture of dialogue and speculation, and the brief line allow variety and much wit and paradox.

After an opening passage of seventeen lines commenting on the seriousness of marriage and pondering what the original Adam and Eve might think of the institution by now, longer passages introduce an Adam and Eve of the present, struggling with the human complexities that, the poem says, psychology cannot explain. Eve is talented, changeable, and is said (in lines reminiscent of Robinson Jeffers, the only such passage in Moore's published work) to be possessed of an almost suicidal beauty. This reflection leads to recollection of her role as "the central flaw" in Eden—as the cause of "that lamentable accident" that exempted Adam from primary blame for man's loss of the Garden, an exemption Moore as a woman makes a point of referring to with sarcasm. Like Eve, Adam has a beauty that, the poem tells us, is properly celebrated in certain works of art. Adam has been a prophet and sage; but he has failed to observe the unpredictable qualities of woman, he has taken an undue pride in the reverence some have paid him, and he has let himself be dazzled into marriage, a state that is a "trivial" source for the disruption of the grand role he has enjoyed.

Once married, a couple finds that the counsels of Hymen, the marriage god, will be of no help. For example, his advice that marriage late in life is best is of little aid to those who presumably have wed at the customary age. Man and wife must recognize that friction is to be expected and perhaps even valued, for it is a way of testing experience; they must learn at some pain the difference between independence and bondage, and they must accept inevitable differences in opinion and in desires. There follows a dialogue between Eve and Adam, each presenting favorite accusations against the other. The conversation ends with the speaker's comment that each loves himself rather too much and that they are "poor" as long as this is true—poor, we may deduce, in peace and in the strength a better understanding of each other could give them.

The concluding issue is stated in the inquiry as to what can be done for such "savages" who frustrate all but the most visionary of those who would like to help them. It is obviously rare that a marriage joins two whole-souled opposites who instead of feuding can reinforce each other. Indeed, so ideal a marriage is so unlikely that the possibility of it is for a moment mocked in lines comparing it to Columbus's demonstration with the egg. Yet, though improbable, such a "charitive Euroclydon," such an impersonal though passionate love, is still the ideal; it would develop a "disinterestedness" that "the world" hates but may nevertheless be found in those with "simplicity of temper." An example appears in an old-fashioned wedding picture. The photographed couple's sturdy individualism of pose, obvious simplicity, and forthright reliance on principle (indicated by a Bible in the foreground) illustrate that paradox verified, so to speak, in the closing lines by allusion to Daniel Webster: the paradox that we must somehow in marriage, as elsewhere, respect and win both liberty and union. The political allusion serves to give the statement application not only to the marriage partnership but to life generally. We must somehow unite in our lives a proper care for the physical with a due recognition for the spiritual in all experience.

"Marriage" is atypical in dealing with an intangible circumstance that Moore could not effectively represent by means of an object or an animal. Possibly because of her "restraint," her desire to keep herself out of the situation, she set down her details with so little explanation that several passages are elliptical. The poem lacks the intensity of, for example, parts of George Meredith's "Modern Love"

series; such intensity, however, might be out of place in what is
essentially a witty, ironically pitying commentary. In such later
poems on the theme of self-discipline as "What Are Years?" and
"Nevertheless" Moore becomes more directly editorial. The subjects
in these poems, however, are simpler. "Marriage" is complex at
least partly because the relationships it discusses are complex.
Critics taking part in or influenced by feminism have given much
attention to this poem. But no one has succeeded in reading it as
a tract on gender relations. Both Eve and Adam are at points mocked,
pitied, and sympathized with. Marriage relationships continued to
interest Moore, who never married. Over thirty years after publishing the poem, she entered in her notebook for 1955–56 this
comment on one couple: "They've been married for some time; don't
hate each other. What can their daydreams be?" Moore does not
explain the remark. Perhaps the implication is that the consuming
daydream of the marriage partner is about a life free from one's
mate. If that is the notion, it shows a cynicism stronger than appears
in the poem.

Since true self-discipline will allow liberty, it is not to mean mere
"neatness of finish." It must embrace diversities, a point illustrated
by the meditation centering on a wild mountain that becomes the
relatively long poem "An Octopus." Here Moore is at her shifting,
allusive best; an extended analysis by Bonnie Costello concludes
aptly that this poem "does not mean, but does."[3] The speaker refers
to the peak once as Big Snow Mountain, but most references are to
guidebooks and pamphlets having to do with Mount Rainier (which,
in the early 1920s, was sometimes called Mount Tacoma—a name
that the poem uses once). Some of the information comes, too, from
experience: Moore and her brother climbed partway up the mountain
in 1922 when he was stationed at a Washington navy base. Though
it is "deceptively reserved and flat," and has arms "misleadingly
like lace," the mountain is an enormous formation of valleys, forests,
glaciers, and snow-dunes; it is home to the porcupine, beaver, bear,
and goat; it meets the demands of weather-beaten roamers, ignorant
tourists, and holidaying businessmen. Nearly four pages of *Complete
Poems* are given to this description, in which the details as usual are
particularized vividly, and such attitudes as irony, sarcasm, and
humor appear in appropriate passages: this is very much a Marianne
Moore mountain, not a guidebook mountain. Just before the one
stanza break, the *Selected Poems* version gave an additional thirty-

two lines. Most of these described flowers found on the mountain; apparently when preparing later books Moore felt that her presentation had a magnitude suited to its subject without these lines. Lines omitted from late printings mentioned the naturalness of a bluejay on the mountain, one element in the description being that the bird knew no Greek. Contrast and comparison between characteristics and activities associated with the mountain and the insistence of the ancient Greeks on what are here represented as light, sophisticated ideas—early printings, indeed, referred to the Greeks as "grasshoppers"—seem meant to highlight the stubborn persistence of the mountain in being exactly what it is.

The Greeks enjoyed "delicate" activities, not invigorating mountain sports; they liked "smoothness," distrusting such complexities as those represented by the varied elements of the mountain and seeking to produce a simple definition of even so elusive a quality as happiness. Their artificial wisdom was "remote" from the practicality displayed by the wardens of the mountain's game preserve—men whose rules forbidding visitors to drink, gamble, or disobey seem a "sarcasm" on the abstract speculations of the Greeks. Yet complexity is essential. It is "self-evident," the poem says, that one must be restrained and obedient to the mountain's requirements if he would match its strength (must be, one might say, Spartan in behavior).

Like Henry James, the mountain is "damned" and neglected by the public because of the rigor of its demands. The public thinks that James tried only for "neatness of finish," failing to see the difference between his "restraint" of passion and a mere decorum. Similarly the public abhors or avoids the mountain because it is not easy of access. It is neither a classic polish nor a crowd-pleasing smoothness that distinguishes the mountain, but "relentless accuracy." The poem ends with nineteen lines vividly particularizing this "accuracy": the mountain's quality of being exactly what it was designed to be, of existing without reference to abstractions or interpretations or judgments that human beings might make from or about it. The mountain is an exemplification of "the thing itself," that which is precisely what its self directs it to be. No mythical Olympus of the gods, it is a realistic, geological mountain in all its mountain-ness.

The need for a discipline that will allow freedom for the self within a spiritual and physical partnership is asserted in "Marriage";

the rigor that preserves wholeness of being is admired in "An Octopus." In "Sea Unicorns and Land Unicorns" Moore combined
allusions to actual and mythical creatures with elements of religious
symbolism to celebrate the unity of the spiritual and the material
that she deemed to be the essence of reality. The first forty-three
lines present and comment upon the "fourfold combination" of land
and sea unicorns and of land and sea lions found on medieval maps
and tapestries as well as in legendry. The sea unicorn (the narwhale
of the Arctic, a tusked whale) and the sea lion are the origin of the
fabulous beasts that decorate ancient marine maps, the poem tells
us; the two creatures are associated in milieu even though the sea
unicorn devours the sea lion. And though the land lion is an enemy
of the land unicorn, legendry says that these beasts also seek out
the same habitats. These associations despite hostility prove a certain
"unanimity," the poem tells us, and lines 23 to 27 observe delightedly the strength that opposing personalities gain through unity.
The creatures, it would seem, have in some respects the kind of
partnerships suggested in "Marriage" as ideal though almost
unattainable.

Unicorns and lions also are frequently associated in embroideries,
especially those making use of the British royal arms (which picture
the unicorn of Scotland facing the lion of England). Like cartog-
raphers' embellishments, these designs are likely to include the sea
unicorn of maritime Britain and the land unicorn English explorers
thought indigenous to the Americas, as well as the sea lion of
Britain's Pacific possessions and the land lion of heraldry. The passage ends with the land varieties of unicorn and lion facing each
other rampant on the tapestry, as they do on the British arms. The
four creatures in their varied combinations make "an odd fraternity."
These combinations, together with the creatures' worldwide range
and the mixture of allusions to the real and the legendary, suggest
that the intention is to represent oneness amid apparent diversity—
an idea linked in Moore's system with unity of physical and spiritual
experience.

The last thirty-eight lines of the poem give a delighted presentation of the land unicorn's magical abilities. The lines open with
a passage making casual reference to the lion of St. Jerome, a beast
associated in legendry with the resurrection of Christ (Moore makes
use of this legendry in her later poem "Leonardo da Vinci's"). The
unicorn can elude all ordinary huntsmen by such feats as throwing

himself head foremost from cliffs. The poem retells the medieval belief that he could be captured only by placing a virgin in the forest to lure him out of hiding. This story was taken to be a parallel to Christian belief; the unicorn represents Christ drawn to the virgin's womb, betrayed and slain by man, but risen again. The land unicorn of Moore's poem thus perhaps represents Christ; the import would be that only the humble and innocent may expect to receive Christ. Because the unicorn or Christ has great strengths, miraculous powers, the ideal union of those seemingly "much opposed" would be a partnership of this figure with the gentle virgin. Since the land unicorn represents the broad range of creatures discussed earlier in the poem, the application is also more general: only the innocent, those with a true humility, may hope to comprehend the fundamental oneness of the spiritual and the material.

That such unity is suggested by harmony with one's milieu is indicated in "The Monkey Puzzle." This name was one sure to interest Moore, especially since it is the appellation of a tree (the "monkey pine" of the Chilean coast). The poem presents the defiant impenetrability, the resistance to straightening, that make the tree seem to have deliberately chosen the loneliness of its environment. No one takes it from its lost woods, though there is a beauty in its "complicated starkness." The real puzzle, however, is neither the tree's twisted form nor its determined resistance and isolation; it is the reason for its existence. No explanation can be given, the poem concludes, because "we prove, we do not explain our birth." Not words but living gives the true exposition of inner nature. Like the cliff in "The Fish" and the mountain in "An Octopus," the tree in its triumph within a harsh environment seems to embody qualities of spirit.

Deliberate variation in style between the first and second stanzas is probably the most noticeable characteristic of "Injudicious Gardening," another poem on the theme of privacy. The notes indicate that the situation parallels or was suggested by an exchange of letters between Robert Browning and Elizabeth Barrett. The reader should observe also the somewhat stronger statement of the second stanza in the earlier version printed in the original *Selected Poems*. The speaker remarks in the first stanza that he will continue to like yellow roses despite the fact that a dictionary of flowers says roses of this color symbolize infidelity. This stanza is simple in diction and in phrasing. The second stanza, however, becomes Latinate and intellectual, a change that offends the usually-approving critic Randall Jarrell (*Poetry and the Age*). The change in style parallels the change in emphasis from the merely aesthetic to the moral. One may disregard supposed symbolism of flower colors, the speaker suggests, because it is an artificial overlay not inherent in the flowers themselves. But the moral world is solidly real. One must take seriously the right of the self to maintain its integrity, to disapprove of what intrudes or affronts.

The thought of the second stanza is as complex as its language. Complexity in thought does not necessarily require complicated expression, but matching expression to content can be a useful poetic device. Moore frequently changed her diction to suit her content; and, as in this poem, she sometimes indicated approval by simplicity and disapproval by complexity. Examples are the variations in "Nothing Will Cure the Sick Lion but to Eat an Ape," and, as Hugh Kenner has noted (in *The Art of Poetry*), those in "The Swan and the Cook" in Moore's *Fables of La Fontaine*.

Moore used one-syllable lines in "To Statecraft Embalmed" to speed the pace of her satire. She made frequent use of such lines in "To Military Progress," with the result that the words seem to drip down the page almost like drops of blood. The poem, a satire on the concept named in its title, scorns it as so stupid that it fails to see its own suicidal nature. This nature is indicated by the picture of military progress gloating even as the battlefield crows feed on its torso. These crows search for "the lost / head ": such progress is, indeed, brainless.

Aesthetics and Behavior

The last nine of the *Selected Poems* pieces, as given in the *Complete Poems* printing, provide a series of comments on aesthetics and on behavior, topics related in Moore's ethics. Such relationships are cited in the opening lines of "An Egyptian Pulled Glass Bottle in the Shape of a Fish." The bottle combines satisfaction of a practical need, the moral quality of "patience" that was necessary in its maker, and the art needed to complete it. It is thus appropriate for celebration by simile and metaphor. In shape it is like a wave, rising to a crest; in color it provides the "spectrum" seen in the scales of a fish. It is an object of obvious attraction for Moore.

Failure to see the perfection of such an object, unless an explicit statement of it is given, is scorned in "To a Steam Roller." The critic, reader, or poet himself who insists on an "application," a direct statement of moral or other meaning, may be said to "lack half wit" and to see no differences among works of art. If it were possible for anyone to be "impersonal," to be dispassionate in aesthetic judgment, it would be such a person. It is not to be expected that this person would be attended by a butterfly, would ever, for example, exhibit a spirit of imaginative independence. Yet if there is such a "complement," such a completion of seemingly dull sensitivity, it is vain to question its "congruence." We may recall the remark at the end of "The Monkey Puzzle" that existence is established not by words but by being.

What the critic should see, we are told in "To a Snail," is that good art results from following inner principle. Being informed by principle, good style is neither ornamental nor accidental. Compression, for example, is a virtue related to modesty. It is, we deduce, a device for achieving the restraint Moore valued. Such a device is not an "acquisition," not a mere "incidental quality"; it is as natural to the work of the inspired artist as the horn of the snail is to its bearer. The tenth line, which seems to apply particularly to Moore's own metrics, says that if "feet" are not present there should be "a method of conclusions." If the poet does not follow a traditional metrical pattern, he must develop another means of giving movement to his presentation; he cannot give a merely static picture.

The critic who perceives well may detect error and yet go too far in his attempts at correcting it. The one-sentence anecdote given in the ten lines of "Nothing Will Cure the Sick Lion but to Eat an Ape" suggests this when it tells of a man who once detected a "hollowness" of attitude—perhaps in certain works of art—that beauty itself could not redeem. But he took a "disproportionate satisfaction" in his discovery; since vanity under any circumstances results in a lack of decorum, he expressed himself in a "denunciatory/upheaval." The result was that, though he correctly condemned a mistake, he succeeded not in restoring usefulness but in smothering his audience with his "fresh air." The title, quoted from Carlyle, is therefore ironic: surely there is a less violent way of curing the illness of the lion. The expression in one sentence does not result in breathlessness, for the length of phrasings and the use of multisyllabled words slow the reader down; at the same time, the grammar produces a desirable tautness in statement.

"To the Peacock of France" shows Molière as a wise artist who perceived the society of his time accurately and did well what was necessary to do. Deducing correctly the pattern his talents would have to follow for him to succeed, he made himself appear an appropriate "golden jay" and took on when necessary even the colors of the clown Scaramouche, a "black-opalescent dye." He was not a libertine, for he only kept pace with the moral expectations of the times; his "first adventure"—probably a reference to his affair with Madeleine Béjart, a woman with whom he was long associated but did not marry—was his own concern, not a matter for the rest of us to judge him on. Allusion to his having in this "adventure" a "repertory" seems to imply that his behavior in it was theatrical. The second stanza asserts that Molière's sensible attitude was also observable in his playwriting. Though as a man of his world he was a "peacock," not an anchorite in a cell, he wrote good plays without "horrifying sacrifice of stringency." He used the theatrical conventions of his time to win favor with the king and, more important, with the public, arousing a "spontaneous" delight by the display of his "broad tail," his showmanship. Frivolity of exterior was a necessary protective device; in adopting it Molière was showing the wisdom of spirit that made him an artist.

A poet who believes in the need for inspiration is likely to hold that fundamental principles of art are much the same regardless of the age one lives in. In "The Past Is the Present" Moore showed her belief that, though style and manner change, there are permanent aesthetic virtues. Since she herself occasionally used "external action" and frequently used rhyme, we are not surprised to find reference to contemporary belief that these qualities may be "effete" and "outmoded" placed in an "if" clause. Conceding that the taste of the moment may oppose them, she will "revert" to Hebrew poetry (a literature she praised in "Novices" for its oceanic virtues). Quoting a speaker who has remarked that Hebrew poetry is "prose with a sort of heightened consciousness," Moore adds that "ecstasy affords/ the occasion" for poetry and that "expediency determines the form." The poet, that is, writes as the result of an inspiration, and he uses whatever form he finds convenient, whether because it has been furnished by a tradition or, as with Moore, has resulted from his own labors. Early versions of the poem had quotation marks around this comment also. Removing them means the remark is presented as the poet's own words, making it seem more persuasive than it did as a report at second hand. Recent printings also omit an italicized introductory stanza that appeared in *Others*.

The revelation afforded by unconscious inspiration is amusingly illustrated in " 'He Wrote the History Book.' " The title quotes a small boy's remark giving a sudden insight into his father's character, casting a ray of "whimsicality" on his father's "mask of profundity." In the 1981 printing the ten lines of the 1951 version are compressed to nine, the "recent occasion" of that version becomes "a Bible class," and the speaker "XY" becomes "the teacher." The boy's reasoning is "synthetic," moving straight to what is to him a reasonable conclusion, and is to us an indication that his father has a touch of whimsy despite his sober exterior.

How whimsicality may mask profundity is a theme of "Sojourn in the Whale," a poem celebrating Ireland as an example of the defiant independence Moore admired in "The Fish" and in "An Octopus." The Irish, she says, often pursue wrong tactics and have long been "swallowed" by the English. They have had to listen to insulting assertions that their country has a weak temperament and that, blind and incompetent, it will eventually be "compelled by experience" to give in to the demands of its conquerors that it accept a status of inferiority because "water seeks its own level." But Ireland, the poem concludes, is not motionless; it will one day overcome the obstacles now facing it and "rise automatically." The title implies that Ireland now is in the situation of Jonah when he was riding about in the whale: it is only temporarily a captive of the English cetacean. And the poem also playfully reminds the reader of more recent traditions of "a Jonah" as a nuisance, if not an outright danger, to those who harbor it. This poem is briefer, less analytical of Irish temperament, and less complex in expression than the later "Spenser's Ireland." When first published (1917), the second stanza's mention of a "feminine temperament" identified with Irish bumbling and whimsy no doubt seemed merely incidental or matter of fact—men, at least, did view femininity as less than logical. In the era of feminism, however, one may be tempted to read the poem as a defense of feminine freedom from male convention.

Selected Poems ended, appropriately enough, with "Silence," an examination of the profundity in decorum. "Superior people," the poem tells us, do not impose on others; they are self-reliant to the point that they can occasionally enjoy solitude, and they have a depth of feeling that causes them to become speechless when someone else's speech has delighted them. This is not "silence," the speaker now decides, but "restraint"; it is not a morose or rude unwillingness to participate, but a decorum that avoids effusions and demands for attention. The last two lines present and comment upon another quotation, "Make my house your inn." This invitation is not "insincere" because "Inns are not residences." That is, the speaker himself exemplifies the kind of restraint he values when inviting others; he makes it civilly clear that their stay is to be for a reasonable period of time. Restraint to Moore meant self-reliance, and it meant thoughtfulness. It was not what Freudians call repression, but rather a discipline making possible the only valid expression of one's self. Restraint in expression was a necessary counterpart to the armoring she recommended, for if one is not to be imposed upon by others he most certainly should not himself make impositions. Restraint, "silence," has even a spiritual function: Moore recommended it in her essay "If I were Sixteen Today" because, she said, if one keeps his tongue still he may hear "promptings from on high."

Discarded Poems

Both the 1951 *Collected Poems* and the 1981 *Complete Poems*—as well as other gatherings—omit four works printed in the 1935 *Selected Poems*. One of these omissions, "Roses Only," seems quite as good as some of the pieces Moore preserved. It has what is, perhaps, too proselike a beginning, and it includes one awkward nominative expression ("the without-which-nothing of pre-eminence"). But it has a clear movement from beginning to end; and, as a treatment of the paradox that beauty is sometimes a liability rather than an asset, that thorns may be the best part of the rose, it is suited to her attitudes and themes.

The other omitted pieces are all somewhat less clear than Moore's usual work. "Is Your Town Nineveh?" gives two stanzas addressed to someone who feels "desolate," who perhaps has been quelled in an attempt to assert a freedom. " 'The Bricks Are Fallen Down . . .' "—the full title has twenty-one words—is a twelve-line piece apparently meant to celebrate a people who, accepting their inability to eliminate war, ceased to fear it. As it stands in *Selected Poems*, it attempts to make its assertion by means of the negative phrasing that was one of Moore's favorite devices for indirection. The negatives in this poem, however, are mistaken: the people, we are told, "did not say" that they would *not* be intimidated by troubles. The words making up the long title of the poem appeared as a passage in another early piece, "Feed Me Also River God," which Moore also discarded. Somewhat tangled negatives again make for difficulty in "Like a Bulrush," the fourth omitted poem; and the nature of its subject is not clear.

Moore omitted from *Selected Poems* itself, and did not later reprint, a number of other poems she published in the years before 1935. Of the thirteen poems she printed in the Bryn Mawr literary magazines *Tipyn O'Bob* and *The Lantern* from 1907 to 1909, she reprinted only "Progress" (in *O to Be a Dragon*), under the title "I May, I Might, I Must"; the poem also appeared in several magazines and anthologies from 1957 to 1970); and "To a Screen-maker" (in *Poems* as "He Made This Screen"); she paralleled the opening lines of one other, "Ennui," in a passage in "The Plumet Basilisk." Moore apparently regarded most of these works as juvenilia. The reader may agree that most have lamenesses in expression.

These poems demonstrate, however, that some of Moore's characteristic concerns developed early. There are poems on pride ("Tunica Pallio Proprior"); on the need for art to be exact in perception ("Qui s'excuse, s'accuse"); and on the superiority of sensory experience to verbalization ("My Senses Do not Deceive Me"). In "Progress" and "Ennui" some of the terseness of expression she later developed is apparent; and in "My Lantern" she experimented with the one-syllable line. But most of the poems are academic imitations of the post-Victorians. We can hardly believe that Moore thought herself to be writing anything other than exercises when she turned out the drinking song "Under a Patched Sail" and the sailor love song "The Sentimentalist."

Experimentation with forms and subjects is also obvious in Moore's early professional verse. There, as in her Bryn Mawr work, she was occasionally susceptible to a neoromantic excess, to prettified fin de siècle rhyming. This flaw is apparent in such work as "That Harp You Play So Well" (1915)—addressed to David the psalmist and filled with phrases like "what boots the art"—and in "Counseil to a Bacheler" (1915), four lines of quasi-Early Modern English. At this period she was not yet always able to achieve a presentation of indirection. Thus "The Wizard in Words" and "George Moore" (both of 1915) fail to convey genuine irony because they rely upon prettiness and polish rather than upon vigorous insight. The irony in "Masks" (1916) is commonplace; a much revised version of this poem, appearing in *Observations* as "A Fool, A Foul Thing, a Distressful Lunatic," is more concrete but it still lacks freshness. The sarcasm of "You Say You Said" (1918) is didactic, and the poem's phrasing is not clear.

The fullest representation of her early work is *Observations* (1924), which reprints most of the verse she had published to that date, including twenty-one of the twenty-four pieces given in *Poems* (1921). *Observations* omits from the works in *Poems* only "To William Butler Yeats on Tagore," "He Made This Screen"—both conventional rhyming pieces—and "Feed Me, Also, River God," which approaches Moore's later stance of careful thoughtfulness but has an uncharacteristically abrupt, almost flippant, ending.

Of the fifty-three poems in *Observations*, most reappear in one or another of Moore's later books. Uncertainties in rhythm, syntax, and attitude doubtless occasioned her decision not to reprint some of the discarded pieces. Thus "Radical" is flat and a bit halting in rhythm; "Reinforcements" is prosaic; "Talisman" may have seemed to Moore herself to falter because of objections Eliot voiced to it in his Introduction to *Selected Poems* (that it is "commonplace" in sentiment and inaccurate in its description of a sea gull). We might wish, on the other hand, that Moore had restored "Dock Rats"; it gives a colorful celebration of sensory delights of place and a comment on the superiority of desires for such experience to motives of "expediency." The poem as it first appeared in Alfred Kreymborg's *Others for 1919* was in a slow-moving five-line stanza; but, as revised to a four-line stanza in *Poems*, it moves with appropriate deftness.

Chapter Three
Armor for Use: Middle Period Poems

Many of the thirty additional poems Moore published in *Collected Poems* of 1951 have as themes discipline and courage, values always honored in her work but perhaps somewhat more on her mind with the approach and subsequent outbreak of World War II. She re-emphasized the need for captivity by strong belief, insisting that only the person possessed by faith can act in freedom, can sustain the discipline necessary for heroic behavior. Changes in emphasis and additions to her ethics do appear, however. In her early work she would sometimes reprove, even scold her fellow human being; now though she continued to keep her guard up, to operate, as one title puts it, "in distrust of merits," she began to consider that perhaps she must go out actively for "Victory" if she was to achieve it. She became less directly corrective, more understanding of people's moral handicaps and thus of their moral possibilities. She still recommended armoring of the self, but this was to be less the aloof defiance represented by the cliff in "The Fish" and more a steeling from within: the whole armor of the Lord, advised in Ephesians, is worn not to enable withdrawal but to fortify endeavor; courage itself becomes a spiritual quality. Finally, in these works of what we may term a middle period, Moore added to her exposition of values three abstract or ultimate qualities she had not dealt directly with before—love, beauty, and spiritual grace. These changes reinforced determination to become more affirmative. They demonstrated greater confidence in the power of poetic exposition and greater assurance in belief.

Changes in style may be both matters of technique and responses to differing needs of expression. In this middle period there is relatively little of the Latinate diction that appeared in some of Moore's early work; the juxtapositions are still clever, but commonly less abrupt; and words very rarely break in the middle to maintain accuracy in syllable count or to achieve a rhyme. The effect of these alterations is to give the poems an air of ease, to intimate a subdued, graceful humor without undue mockery or irony. Though the style retains its cleverness and its wit, these poems do not defy; their tone is that of a quietly reasonable invitation to take part in a consideration of the subject. But these qualities may also be found in some of her early poems; their dominance in this period does not necessarily represent so much a change in stylistic principles as a shift in strategy.

She does in these poems sometimes give more direct editorial comment. In *Selected Poems* the typical work was tied to one bird, beast, cliff, or other "object"; the poem developed in terms of this, by analogy with it and allusion to it. Even in such fairly complex poems as "Nine Nectarines" and "The Plumet Basilisk" the consideration was associated firmly with a particular set of objects. But now she sometimes—as in the title poems "What Are Years?" and "Nevertheless"—would break away from attachment to a "thing." Passages in both these poems allude to a variety of objects that serve a purpose at the moment; both poems ground their cautionary generalizations firmly in sensory realities, but neither allows one object or set of objects to govern its expression. Even in such a less urgent poem as "Rigorists," the "thing," the reindeer, functions as a source for allusions but does not govern the poem. Moore's frequent comments keep us from letting presentation of the creature dominate our minds. The very titles suggest the change. *Observations* indicated poetry making a comment based upon a perceived thing; but *What Are Years* raises an abstract question, and *Nevertheless* seems to suggest continuation of a meditation.

Years: An Opportunity

The first volume of this period was *The Pangolin and Other Verse* (1936); but, since all four of its poems reappeared in *What are Years* (1941), they may conveniently be considered part of it. All of the fifteen poems in *What Are Years* had previously been published in magazines or books. The third volume of this period was *Nevertheless* (1944). In *Collected Poems* (1951) Moore also printed nine poems of these years that had not appeared in books.

That life is a moral experience best confronted with courage is the suggestion of the opening lines in the title poem "What Are Years?" Being only human, we are "naked," we have an "innocence" that leaves us open to error. If our condition is a plight, we never-theless endure it because we have courage, the heroism to survive and to be "glad" though in "resolute doubt" and even in defeat. Such courage, a quality more spiritual than physical, arises from the will. It is a choice one makes; it is the vision of the man who "accedes to mortality," not as a coward, but as one who recognizes that his human condition is an entrapment from which there is no escape for him as a living being. Yet he struggles because he knows too that he possesses a spirit that demands heroic behavior of him. "Mortality" lies about us; yet, like the waves of the sea, we survive because we continue to struggle.

The human being who feels strongly thus "behaves" heroically. Like the bird who sings though caged, he will get along without "satisfaction"—the relatively trivial delights of an impossible free-dom—because he can live in "joy" of spirit. To give in, to become cowed, would be to accept mere "mortality"; to behave heroically is to recognize eternity, is to respond to the more than mortal spirit within us. "Years," then, are a chance to build mettle, to prove in action the inspirations of spirit.

The theme of struggle as essential, of the trapped paradoxically being free, is most fully treated in "What Are Years?" but is common in Moore's work, especially in the poems of this book. Thus "Spen-ser's Ireland" tells us that one is not free till he has been captured by belief; and "The Paper Nautilus" speaks of being "hindered to succeed." Moore herself (in Whit Burnett, editor, *This Is My Best*, 1942) spoke of "What Are Years?" as "elegiac," as a commentary upon the realization that even the most vigilant strugglers may lapse but that all may be "redeemed into inviolateness" by a sufficient courage. Its emphasis on bravery of spirit despite "mortality" is perhaps what led Ezra Pound to read it at a memorial service for Moore after her death in 1972.

In quite another context, yet similar in quality, are the values honored in "Rigorists," a poem remarking on the "reprieve" from starvation given to Eskimos in 1891 by a shipment of reindeer. These animals are examples of the "unconscious fastidiousness" Moore praised in "Critics and Connoisseurs." Their adaptations to the rigors of their Lapland environment make them perfectly disciplined in body and spirit. Human artists may depict a decorative reindeer, but the real animal is itself a "queen of alpine flowers" and an "ornament" while at the same time a lion in strength. In this

purposeful though unconscious beauty lay the promise of salvation
for the Eskimo, a promise acted upon by the "quiet" educator
Sheldon Jackson.
Moore relied in "Rigorists" on extreme simplicity of form. The
first six stanzas are presented as a quotation of a friend's description
of the animals—a device, as in "Silence," that allows the poet to
interpret descriptive details without seeming overly didactic. The
last three stanzas then quietly marvel at the point that this creature
of legend and ornament was in real life a savior. It is as though the
reindeer is so good, even so obvious, an example of the beauty
arising from purposeful strength that neither analysis nor commentary is necessary; the poet to make her point need only present useful
details in an ordering as uncomplicated as the animal itself.

Advocacy of morally disciplined behavior, of rigorous adjustment
to necessity, is not meant to deny the importance of freedom for
the spirit. Celebration of this freedom is the theme of "Light Is
Speech," a poem making traditional associations of France with
frankness and of speech with the light of inspiration or spirit. The
situation is that of the time of publication in early 1941. France
had been conquered by the Nazis; the northern and western portions
of the country were held by a German army of occupation, and the
central and southern areas were ruled by a German-directed government at Vichy. "Speech" and "light" still reinforce each other,
the first sentence assures us; they still are honorable when French
in origin. The war, that is, has not erased the contributions of
France to civilized man. We are to recall cocky Nazi threats, mentioned in a magazine article Moore quotes later in the poem, that
conquered nations would not be denied the blessings of illiteracy.
Light still comes from the sun and the stars; it is in itself a "language," speaking to us of the values we associate with the name
France. A lighthouse designed to be visible by both ships and planes
is the symbolic descendant of such spokesmen for France as Voltaire,
Montaigne, and the philologist Emile Littré.

The lighthouse is "defenseless," and Voltaire and Montaigne spoke
out against odds. We English-speaking peoples, spared the invasion
France had undergone, heard a spokesman for France demand, in
character, that the truth be told even though it is unpleasant. The
demand is quoted from Marshal Pétain, the soldier who had been
a hero in World War I but in 1941 was regarded by the Free French
and by the anti-Axis countries as a traitor because he was serving

as head of the Vichy government. The ending, therefore, would appear to be ironic. In asserting that we can only reply that France means "enfranchisement," a country that will " 'animate whoever thinks of her,' " the poem seems to be replying that France should stand not for the duplicity apparent at Vichy but for the values traditionally associated with her name.

France should have the courage to stand for values. The results and benefits of courage are subjects of the next three poems. "He Digesteth Harde Yron" gives an example of the heroic that has survived barbarisms that killed others of its type. This is the "camel-sparrow" or ostrich. Rightly admired for his devotion to his young and for the value of even his plumes, this bird, the poem suggests, could hardly be expected to honor the men who in bygone days treacherously costumed themselves in his plumage in order to sneak up on and kill him. The contrast between the naturalness of an animal and the artificiality of men is similar to that drawn in "The Jerboa."

The next several lines, through the short sixth stanza, marvel over the ostrich's movements and the appropriateness of his role as a figure in legendry. (Late printings omit two and a half stanzas which gave extra detail on the bird's methods of escape and his skill at running.) Stanza 7 lists specific examples of waste, or worse. Yet the lavish but revolting banquet on ostrich brains and the ugly goblets referred to, indicate in a perverse way the human recognition of the justice and the genuineness the bird represents. They "dramatize a meaning" which is "always missed" by the man who sees only the misuse itself—the "externalist" who fails to see that unconcious respect for the bird causes man to choose it for his mistaken attention.

The power of the ostrich lies in his invisible spirit; even where there is no "freedom," his "so-called brute" courage knows this. The "heroism" the ostrich practiced to survive prevented the fate that overtook birds possessing more of "grandeur" but less of courage. His spirit, his courage of the invisible, has made the ostrich a creature capable of arousing respect and wonder. He is properly a symbol of justice, for by his courage he earned the survival he has achieved. Like the hero in "What Are Years?" who endured in his entrapment because he would not cower, the ostrich survives because he rebels against the "greed" that surrounds him: he feeds his spirit on the hard iron of his discouragements. The *What Are Years* printing employed an eight-line stanza; later printings compressed the material to seven lines, slowing the pace a bit and making the poem seem more meditative. Further compression reduced two of the stanzas in the 1981 printing to six lines each.

A defense of American ways appears in "The Student," once printed together with "The Steeple-Jack" and "The Hero" under the collective title "Part of a Novel, Part of a Poem, Part of a Play." ("The Student" was originally the second of the three sections, but there is no reason to suppose that Moore meant for it to be more of "a Poem" than either of the others.) The student is "a variety / of hero," the person who stands by his opinions, works selflessly, and has a profundity of feeling that may not be apparent on the surface—qualities that make him, like the figure admired in "The Hero," an ideal citizen of Moore's community. He represents that national spirit which, though perhaps not given to recognizing need for rigor, does democratically see education as a path to both knowledge and liberty. The poem paraphrases and quotes approvingly Emerson's essay "The American Scholar."

One necessity for courage is understanding of one's circumstances. In "Smooth Gnarled Crape Myrtle" the object is a tree, perhaps the artificial one of a floral display, or even a painted one. At any rate, it is properly stiff of leaf, rounded, and covered with flowers of pink and blue. That it is both smooth and gnarled makes it appropriate for the discoveries of paradox the poem is to make. Hopping about on the tree, seeming to be "askew" in this regularity, is a smooth, greenish bird, perhaps a female cardinal. The bird is "businesslike," apparently paying no heed to a companion. Between these two, weighting the twig which bears this "peculiar/bouquet," a male cardinal has lit. There should be here, the second stanza comments, some bird from legendry; the cardinal, in his fiery coloring and without the mate one expects him to have, looks out of place; he is a gnarl in the smooth scene.

He is also a disturber of intellectual complacencies. Sight of him, and of the female bird's detachment from him, calls to mind a sewing-box under which is a motto indicating that the conjunction of a pair of painted lovers is intended to illustrate friendship and love. But the picture and motto are a product of "artifice," always a bad quality in Moore's opinion. Indeed, "Art is unfortunate": the picture and motto tell a lie. At least, they are not representative of the relationship between the male cardinal and the other birds in the crape myrtle tree.

Misunderstanding causes society at times to perceive an innocent bachelor to be a rake like a character in a Restoration drama. But the cardinal without a mate—"Rosalindless"—has come near other creatures without ulterior motives even though, ironically, he has lit on the myrtle which in some cultures has been a symbol of love. He has the hard wisdom that keeps him from assuming acceptance by others. The profundity of his comprehension is indicated by the remark that he does not sing but merely "says" what he knows, that he will cling to loneliness because without this feeling he would be more lonely still. Perhaps if he were to associate closely with others he would have to give up some of himself, be a less independent being, and thus be more truly lonely than he is in dignified isolation.

The cardinal's wisdom makes nonsense of the sentimental motto on the box; and it makes even more foolish the similar inscription recalled from an Elizabethan title page which avers that peace brings plenty and that wisdom brings peace. The last word in the poem, "Alas!", is the pet's comment on the folly of this pseudo-wisdom. It is a shame, she seems to say, that this is not so; but truth does not lie in such tidbits from the wishful thinking of self-deceiving humans. It is to be found in the hard knowledge expressed by the cardinal. He has the courage to accept the wisdom that says one must be wary of companionship. He may draw near to others, but he will not surrender himself to them.

The ostrich and the cardinal demonstrate that maturity requires acceptance of a "hard iron." That acknowledgment of responsibility for others makes necessary an equally stern discipline, is shown in "Bird-Witted." Three young mockingbirds seem large enough to care for themselves, but they still depend on their mother, even to the point that one who drops a morsel of food waits for the mother to pick it up for him. These young are indeed "bird-witted" in the usual meaning of the term—unable to care for themselves, too ignorant to recognize the danger of an approaching cat. The mother, however, is "bird-witted" in quite another sense. Accepting her duty to her young, and of necessity taking a serious view of life, she no longer sings the "delightful" notes of her pre-motherhood days; now that she is "astute," her voice has become "harsh."

Though without hope of reward for her effort, except that of continued toil to fill the hungry mouths of her young, the mother bird, made brave by sight of the intruding cat, swoops down and "half kills" him. The cat is "intellectual," he acts "cautiously"; his scheming is an example of the artifice scorned in "Smooth Gnarled Crape Myrtle." The mother bird, in contrast, acts out of an unconscious courage and self-discipline. Her behavior is prompted by maturity of spirit. The poem is faintly reminiscent of "The Frigate Pelican" in *Selected Poems*, but the pelicans were admirable for the adaptation to their environment that permitted them to save themselves from an approaching python; in "Bird-Witted" the admiration is for courageous action on behalf of others. The contrast is indicative of the difference between the first and middle periods of Moore's work.

Ostrich, cardinal, and mockingbird all exemplify the maturity that is the reward of courage. Part of the answer to the query "What are years?" seems to be that they are an opportunity for the individual of armor and restraint to develop a wisdom that will enable one to comprehend and even to grow strong on the hard iron life offers us.

Some of Moore's impressions of the cardinal and the mockingbird came while she was visiting her brother, who in the 1930s was stationed at Norfolk, Virginia. Moore wrote to Bryher on 9 August 1934 to express her delight at the southern scene (among the pleasures was seeing three mockingbird fledglings "persecute their mother for food," a sight that it may be assumed was the source of a passage in "Bird-Witted"). Virginia also gave Moore material for other poems, especially for "Virginia Britannia."

The three poems centered on birds address the behavior of representative heroic individuals. Both "Virginia Britannia" and "Spenser's Ireland" deal with the nature of whole societies over considerable periods of time; both are excellent examples of Moore's mature use of descriptive poetry. In "Virginia Britannia" details of the scene are so abundant that they almost drown out any indication of sociomoral significance. Yet the detail expresses Moore's excited delight that is also part of her comprehension. The sociomoral is not in itself a "message" summing up the poem; it is rather a reminder that, even as Adam and Eve, Americans have not always lived up to the Edenic. Moore wanted to convey exuberance of feeling; the sociomoral was a necessary but secondary component of her comprehension. "Virginia Britannia" explores the connections among the Virginia countryside, the Indians, and the early white settlers. Combining straightforward statement with humor and indignation, the poem speculates on the presence in this environment of foolish and at times wicked human actions, as well as of amusing if misguided aspirations. Its assertions are direct, but are so carefully embedded in details that they seem a part of the poem's texture. Half of the tenth stanza, for example, is a statement that man in Virginia has lacked "mercy." But the reader has been so thoroughly prepared by illustrations implying this point that the comment seems not an intrusion but an inevitable recognition of fact. The poem is concentrated and fresh in syntax without being abrupt. All later printings compress into twelve-line and thirteen-line stanzas material that in the *What Are Years?* printing took seventeen lines; as in "He Digesteth Harde Yron," the change is an improvement, the compactness slowing the pace to match the thoughtfulness of the content. The reader, incidentally, will notice that the crape myrtle, ostrich, cardinal, and mockingbird of the three poems preceding this one all reappear in it.

After detailing some of the Old Dominion scene, Moore mentions a few of the evidences of early settlement that remain. These include the remark on a settler's tombstone that "a great sinner lyeth here," a thought that is quaint in effect at this point, but is suggestive of the poem's attitude toward the history of Virginia's colonization. The man who would admit to sin was "unusual," we are told. Thought of this brings up the incongruity of Captain John Smith's company as well as of some of the early Indians. The careful formality the English on one occasion employed in crowning an Indian chief suggests the care that has produced in "unEnglish" Virginia luxuriant growths of the wall rose and the yew.

But neither Indian nor settler represents the true spirit of the land. The fourth stanza calls on us to observe "the terse Virginian," the mockingbird that here is a creature of mettle who can adopt the guise of any native bird or with insouciance dominate an English garden pedestal. The suggestion seems to be that the bird is the true life of Virginia, that in a guarded defiance he frequents man's habitations, watching with a self-assurance born of his knowledge that he is the permanent heir of the land. The bird is seen sitting in the garden of a country home, perhaps in Williamsburg. Pansies that bloom there in splendid but short-lived pride are, it is implied, an emblem of all antebellum Virginia where settlers in "establishing the Negro"—as a slave, we recall—were importing an "inadvertent ally," an enemy of tyranny. Settlers who were as odd as the Indians

they conquered; blacks who were to help overcome the social system
that had imprisoned them—Virginia has been, indeed, an "incon-
sistent flower-bed." Some of the oddities, some of the paradoxes in
Virginia floriculture illustrate the point; and these are paralleled by
half-amusing, half-puzzling comparisons between an Indian princess
and an English girl and by the intermixture even yet of Indian and
English names.

Mention of aristocratic names given to frontier counties recalls
the contrasting "tactless" defiance of an early American patriot flag;
this contrast brings to mind such oddities as the combination of
"cotton-mouth snakes and cotton-fields," and the "serpentine" shape
of a beautiful wall. Such incongruities are emblematic of the state's
history. There has been, it is now asserted, some cruelty in all "our"
efforts—all the exploration, imperialism, and colonizing of Europe-
born civilization. Mercy has not been a leading characteristic of
"us." And the Indian, despite his fearsome reputation, was not all
cruelty. Realization that the vaunted white civilization was frequently cruel, the condemned Indian society often magnanimous,
is associated with the paradox that the supposed luxuries of the
civilized settlers were "stark" in comparison with the attributes
Virginia already had—the seemingly drab hedge-sparrow, for example, which sings in "ardor" his "ecstatic" joy. Moore humorously
specifies in the eleventh stanza, and verifies in her notes to the
poem, the point that this remarkable avis "wakes up seven minutes
sooner than the lark."

The touch of humor is purposeful, for the poem is not to turn
into a defense of Indians and an attack on whites. Native and English
flora have by now become indistinguishable, the last stanza tells us;
there is no longer any point in dwelling upon whatever differences
may once have existed. Over all the scene and over the continuing
assertiveness of the Virginia town—whose inhabitants, we may
assume, include whites, blacks, and whatever Indians survive—the
clouds expand to dwarf the "arrogance" of mankind, the pride that
prevented men from seeing the possibilities Virginia offered. By
their grandeur and their suggestion that other possibilities await
man's discovery, the clouds give an "intimation of what glory is."
The theme of despoliation, at least of failure to see the true possibilities of a land, links the poem to "The Plumet Basilisk" and to
"The Jerboa."

Virginia, Moore's speaker holds, is, like all of America, a land of possibilities that wasteful mankind has not yet comprehended. Failure to develop possibilities is also examined in "Spenser's Ireland." This poem muses half-humorously about the obduracy remarked upon in Spenser's "A View of the State of Ireland," a stubbornness Moore's poem finds still to be observed in Ireland. The characters in Spenser's dialogue were puzzled by Irish refusal to submit even to laws which, at least in the view of the conquering English, were intended for their own peace and good order. Moore somewhat similarly viewed the Irish as examples of those who fail to see that freedom comes only with discipline and belief.

Though "Spenser's Ireland" talks of customs now abandoned, it deliberately uses present-tense verbs to suggest that the spirit of obduracy with which these behaviors were associated in the times of Spenser still exists. Thus the poem says that the Irish are "natural"—an adjective having, it seems, both the modern meaning "undisciplined" and the Shakespearian (and Spenserian) sense "foolish." By way of illustrating this, the poem mentions the cloak or mantle with its long, useless sleeves that Spenser's observers found distasteful in the sixteenth century (they believed it was a hiding place for lawbreakers). The idea surely is not to say that the Irish today garb themselves in mantles, but rather to intimate that the spirit that once made them cling to the garment despite English objections is still alive.

The poem opens with lines that present the characteristics summed up in the word "natural." Unchanging Ireland is kind; but it is also "green," this adjective perhaps referring both to the colors of the land and to the immaturity of its inhabitants. The Irish respond neither to scoldings nor to blows, but are easily hurt if not spoken to; they are, indeed, scarcely adult. The second stanza remarks on the legend that, to charm away supernatural intruders, the Irish play the harp backwards and that, to attain invisibility and thus elude giants, they swallow fern seed. Might there not be, it asks, some magical device for unlearning obduracy and thus restoring the "enchantment" of an Ireland unspoiled by the stubbornness of its people? Representative of Irish pigheadedness are the grandmothers who appear in place of mothers in Irish stories of "hindered" characters: the distant past rules Irish life.

Whoever maintains so rigorous an attitude fails to see that freedom—of spirit, we gather—comes only to the person who is the "captive" of "supreme belief," to the one who, we may paraphrase, has the discipline of attitude and behavior that Moore thought belief affords. This trust in the necessity and virtue of faith is not "credulity," the poem continues. The devotee of sport fishing who is a craftsman at tying flies has the pride that rightfully comes from such care: he is not a victim of "madness," at least not insofar as his pride is owing to his skill. (By alluding to the art of fly-tying Moore picked an apt modern parallel to the magical crafts of earlier centuries.) Hands of those who agree that accuracy of performance is valuable produce the leatherlike Irish damask which is so fine as to be watertight. But less carefully crafted art—the poem mentions jewelry that is illustrated in a *National Geographic* magazine article referred to in the notes—is not so beautiful as the bloom of the fuchsia, a product of Irish nature.

Spenser's characters speculated on whether the stubbornness of the Irish arose from something in the stars or in the soil. The speaker similarly speculates on whether the idea of Eire—an independent Ireland—and the birds that seem to represent the spirit of the country indicate an inextricable pigheadedness in the nature of Ireland. If so, she asserts, let them be like Gerald, eleventh Earl of Kildare, who according to Irish horror stories changed himself into various animal forms—let them, that is, be transformed into something else. And then, like one of the Irish enchanters of old, she wishes away these indications of Irish perversity.

Yet the poem must close on a half-ironic, half-humorous note, for Moore was aware of her own distant Irish ancestry. Her speaker wishes she could believe the sentimental assurance of the *National Geographic* writer that the Irish will share one another's troubles, for she, herself Irish, is "dissatisfied." Ireland is still, it would appear, that land of unending resistance that troubled Spenser. The poem's warning and its chiding of the Irish, we may take it, are really directed at the refusal of stubborn men everywhere to recognize the need for the discipline Moore thought belief can give. The poem's presentation of the errors in stubbornness is the counterpart, of course, of the praise she gave Irish fortitude in "Sojourn in the Whale."

To see that the accuracy afforded by repetition is an object of Moore's practice, we need only observe how she repeats her carefully patterned stanza forms throughout a poem. It is not surprising to find her basing a poem—"Four Quartz Crystal Clocks"—on a report that four quartz vibrators kept at even temperature independently maintain the same time and thus provide a standard against which clocks may be checked. Nor is it surprising to find her mentioning that these furnish accurate time for the media of communication, the channels which should convey truth. We know, she remarks, such a historical truth as the fact that Napoleon is dead; and we also know such a scientific truth as the fact that the vibrations of quartz prisms will vary if the temperature changes.

The conjunction of the historical and the scientific seems to suggest that Moore saw one order of time and truth. Thought of the "repetition" of temperature suggests the "accuracy" that should characterize the procedure of the scientist. In a technique similar to that she employed in "Virginia Britannia" Moore's speaker darts back to her store of examples of the quality she would illustrate, rather than giving a rationalistic analysis of it. One can "see," she remarks, that an aye-aye is not a potto, that a bell-boy is not a buoy-ball (she says parenthetically that he should not let himself be embarrassed by punning remarks on the similarity in names), and that glass eyes are not eyeglasses. Even such repetitions should contribute not to confusion but to accuracy, she says. There is a wink in her eye, of course, for in her punning she is taking advantage of possible confusions.

And "you realize," she says in her tone of pleasant reasonableness, that, when you hear the telephone company time announcement (dialed, significantly, by means of a repetitious number), what you are hearing is Jupiter praising "punctuality." The reference to Jupiter perhaps is intended to allude to his identification in myth as the spirit of air, for it is air that is vibrated to produce the sound we hear. In a rather complicated piece of punning etymology the speaker also suggests that the name Jupiter is derived from the French *jour* for day and the Latin *pater* for father. At any rate, Jupiter functions as the god of day and is said to be the son of Father Time, of that Chronos who once ate most of his other children (all but air, water, and the grave, these being three that time cannot devour). Jupiter as the air, the message from the vibrating quartz prisms, is thus telling Father Time himself that punctuality "is not a crime," but is in fact a virtue. This conclusion in which the action turns back upon itself is, of course, apt evidence of the ability of repetition to insist upon meaning. The last line as it appeared in the poem's original printing in 1940 read "is not now a crime." The "now" seemed to suggest a limit to the time during which accuracy has

been valued; omitting it, as later printings do, makes it possible
to think of accuracy as a permanent value.

Necessities: Grace and Love

Moore also employed the descriptive mode in "The Pangolin,"
her fullest statement on relationships among the animal, human,
and spiritual kingdoms. Despite the humorous recognition of her
own affection for such creatures as the pangolin in the exclamation
"Another armoured animal," Moore's real subject is the nature of
man, that animal for whom no physical armoring is adequate. The
pangolin, indeed represents the perfection of the courage and restraint Moore valued; he has the "unconscious fastidiousness" praised
in "Critics and Connoisseurs" and the naturalness admired in "The
Jerboa." But something more than these qualities is needed. "The
Pangolin" shows that the something more is grace, an inspiration
from a spiritual world. The poem also gives Moore's fullest statement
on mankind. It finds us half-comical, half-contemptible, and yet
treats us warmly because, though we lack the perfection of the
animal, we have greater possibility.

Of the poem's nine stanzas, the first five are devoted to an appreciative detailing of the pangolin's characteristics; the last four
stanzas cautiously compare and contrast man with these. The careful
presentation of the animal's armoring and strategems gives concrete
ground for the delight expressed in him; it also provides a listing
of features useful for the parallelism with man. Continuing the
admiration of repetition given in "Four Quartz Crystal Clocks," the
poem celebrates the repetition of pattern in the pangolin's scales.
Occasionally it matches such repetition in its own style. Thus a list
of elements the pangolin may exclude from his nest is given as a
series of nouns linked by "and" rather than by punctuation; the
sculptures on a cathedral are said to include "monk and monk and
monk"; and the last stanza describes the succession of days as "new
and new and new." Those with an interest in style should note the
various changes in wording and punctuation in the different printed
versions of the poem.

The pangolin—the scaly anteater of Africa and Asia—is, we are
told, wonderfully made; like Leonardo da Vinci, he is both artist
and engineer. Armor seems unnecessary on so finely wrought a
creature; yet, considering that he at times becomes covered with

ants, it is good that he is so securely fashioned that he can make even his eyes impenetrable. When endangered, he does not fight; but, with the grace of Westminster Abbey ironwork—an allusion that introduces an association of grace and cathedrals to be developed in later stanzas—he withdraws or rolls himself into a ball. Even this is not the limit of his resources for security, for he has "sting-proof scales" and he can retreat into a rock-lined nest. Indeed, he has developed a virtually absolute restraint; he can shut out "Sun and moon and day and night and man and beast"—elements and considerations that man "in all his vileness" does not have the power to exclude. Each of these has a "splendor," an "excellence"; mention that the animal can escape them but that man cannot, suggests the theme that is soon to become apparent: the animal though admirable in himself is, after all, limited; man, being more greatly gifted, also faces, and must accept, greater responsibilities and challenges. Perfection of restraint is not an ethical goal for a human being.

The pangolin is in his own element a creature filled with fear, yet fearsome in his turn. More elaboration upon the marvels of his protective stratagems leads to the thought of his "not unchain-like machine-like / form." This form is perceived as appropriate to the "creep" of a creature that has been made graceful by the difficulties it meets. From that thought it is an easy transition in the sixth stanza to a consideration of grace as evidenced in some of man's works. Since Moore's speaker chooses to illustrate this quality by remarking upon the artistry of cathedrals, the reader is carried quickly into a meditation upon spiritual grace. In a few lines the poem has moved from the physical to the aesthetic and thence to the spiritual.

The pangolin developed his delightful gracefulness because of the adaptation of his form to his functions; he is designed to meet successfully "adversities, conversities." To explain grace requires "a curious hand." We are then given what is indeed a curious, though appropriate, working out of the idea: if it were not for the fact of immortality, the poem asks, would the engineer-artists who built great cathedrals have "slaved" to associate representations of grace with illustrations, so to speak, of kindliness, of long-enduring time, and of sin being cured? Because these men who were representatives of the central culture of their time had faith in immortality, they could believe in the idea of a grace that incorporated these concepts. Their belief made itself evident in their art, with its rows of grave monks and its graceful mullions. To find grace in a human construction is not unusual, it is suggested; for a sailboat, an example of gracefulness, was man's "first machine."

Like the sailboat, the pangolin moves quietly and is a model of "exactness"; thought of his occasional humanlike "postures" brings the poem back again to man. Less well, if less narrowly, adapted to his functions, man misses half of what he sets out to find; he is complex, embodying in one being a variety of functions that in the animal kingdom are distributed among many creatures. Though, or because, he is relatively infinite in capacity—he may, for example, appear in any stage of dress from the "bedizened" to "stark" nudity—man is as yet far from the perfection achieved by creatures whose possibilities are more limited. Thus man, the "writing master," the self-conscious intelligence of this world, claws out (as might a griffon, a fabulous monster) such quasi-philosophical crypticisms as "Like does not like like that is obnoxious," and misspells the word "error" itself. One must keep a sense of humor when considering such an animal. Though "unignorant," having the gift of a certain intelligence and self-knowledge, man fails in his attempt to pose as unemotional because he is "all emotion." There is hope for him because he has "power to grow," but in his present stage one had best be wary of him.

The pangolin, not being self-conscious, is fearful or fearsome as instinct directs; man, being aware of self, is either boastfully unafraid or a coward. A mammal, not so separate from the pangolin as he might like to think, man retreats like an animal to his abode. But it is no secure pangolin nest, for manufactured habiliments are his only armor. Night is the pangolin's time of greatest activity; but man, in some ways a counterpart of the animal, is "thwarted by the dusk"—darkness for him, we may deduce, being a depression of spirit. The animal accepts calmly the days and nights as they come to him; man, the creature of less perfection but more diversity, finds that each return of day is a new emotional experience. He never learns that naturalness of attitude that, inborn in the animal, enables it to function without some of the fears and foolishness that afflict man himself. Yet in the possibility of renewal, the fact of diversity, lies hope for this imperfect creature, man. This renewal comes with each sunrise, for each day brings a resurrection and a possibility of new grace. The man of this poem is the man of "What Are Years?": he is defeated, but he goes on trying.

The leading issue for *What Are Years* is indicated by its title poem's consideration of the elements in heroic behavior. That poem and the succeeding ones present these elements as courage, self-discipline based on belief, such aesthetic values as craftmanship and accuracy, and the need for grace. What secures and fortifies all these as well as associated requirements is suggested in "The Paper Nautilus," the closing poem, which asserts that "love" is "the only fortress/strong enough to trust to."

The female of the paper nautilus, a mollusk related to the squid and the octopus, raises its young carefully in a thin, glasslike shell. The poem opens with assertions that she does not exercise this care for commercial reasons, nor for the delight of inobservant writers (we may suspect a sarcastic dig at the easy moralizing of Oliver Wendell Holmes's famed "The Chambered Nautilus"). This "perishable" shell is a "souvenir of hope" because it houses the eggs; the nautilus guards it by cradling it in her eight arms. A complicated parallel now first remarks that Hercules in his struggle with the hydra found that his strength was renewed by anger when he was bitten by Cancer, the crab and one of the hydra's supporters; it then implies that, in a similar paradox, the nautilus and its shell become free when the new-hatched young they have guarded struggle free from their supervision. The success of the hatching makes it appear that the guarding arms of the nautilus had intelligence, that they knew the singular value of love as "the only fortress." Perhaps the nautilus is only a creature of instinct, but its behavior nevertheless provides a lesson for man.

The ethical presentation of the poem arises with a seemingly casual grace out of a citation of exact details of the subject, rather than by the easy and obvious analogy that Holmes used. The result is a fine demonstration of how a poem may convey a statement without surrendering to didacticism.

Nevertheless: Be Wary

Moore's next volume, an even slimmer one, brought together in 1944 under the title *Nevertheless* six poems originally published in magazines in the early 1940s. The title seems to indicate that these pieces qualify the assertions of *What Are Years*. Since most of them repeat her usual emphases on courage, craftsmanship, and honesty toward oneself, we may deduce that, though in *What Are Years* Moore gave primary value to grace and love, she did not want her reader to think she was concerned only with such gentle ultimates: courage and the values associated with it remain the immediate necessities.

First in order is the poem labeled on original publication "It Is Late, I Can Wait" but now titled "Nevertheless." It seems in particular a continuation, almost a qualification, of the assertion in "The Paper Nautilus" that love is the only trustworthy fortress. Nevertheless, this poem seems to say, courage is primary for survival. The poem presents a series of examples of courageous behavior in the face of great difficulty: the strawberry that manages to appear a work of art even when torn open; the apple-seeds that are neatly patterned, though locked in place; the roots of the dandelion rubber plant that survive in frozen ground; the prickly pear leaf that, though caught on barbed wire, sends a shoot down to earth. All these, we note, are examples of victory within captivity; like Hercules in "The Paper Nautilus," they may be described as "hindered to succeed." They serve as examples from the plant world of the possibility of winning survival despite, even because of, captivity—the possibility which on the level of ideas is cited in "Spenser's Ireland" and "What Are Years?"

These examples of heroic behavior demonstrate the need for resolute action: they show that "Victory won't come/to me unless I go/to it." As usual in Moore's work, this message—if we may term it that—is not elaborated upon by methods of prose analysis and explication; instead, it is followed immediately by yet another example of courageous endeavor: the grape tendril, which, by knotting and reknotting, chokes an intruding twig. By means of courage, indeed, the weak can overcome his feebleness; the strong can master himself. The poem ends with a final example of "fortitude": the cherry stem that, despite its fragility, has conveyed to the fruit the necessary sap. The "love" cited in "The Paper Nautilus" as the ultimate value is, of course, an ideal; but the importance of courage is "nevertheless" not to be forgotten.

The determined, indeed, are the best associates, or so "The Wood-Weasel" tells us. At least, this is true of those who, like the creature of the title, have a sense of humor in their situation. There is humor in the poem's opening remark that the creature "emerges daintily," a remark which postpones mention of the animal's common designation, skunk. We are told that he is both black and white, that he wears "goat-fur," and that he is "wood-warden"—all details that suggest some association of the humble skunk with Pan, lord of woods and animals. In his white-black wool—repeated emphasis on the colors of his coat seems to reinforce the suggestion of resemblance to Pan, the goat-man—he is truly the "totem," the symbol of determination. Though considered an outlaw, he conducts himself as a chief; and he is capable of any required self-defense. Yet he is "playful." He is, indeed, an altogether admirable model. (The poem was written as a tribute to Moore's friend Hildegarde Watson. Reading from the bottom up, the first letters of the lines spell her name.)

Fortitude and determination are two of the qualities of wisdom. "Elephants" is another of Moore's poems in which the well-defended exemplify wisdom. The poem opens with a scene of two elephant trunks locked in a wrestling match. Since the forces are equal, the picture is almost a still-life; it is an emblem of that unity, that blending of what are in some aspects the opposed, which is one theme of the poem. The elephants, we are told, are not fighting seriously; their match is something of "a pastime." Stanzas 3 through 6 present another instance of a unity of seeming opposites: the picture of a mahout asleep cradled in the hollow of his sleeping elephant's body. The elephant is "unconscious" of the man's weight, and the man's pose indicates he feels as secure as though he were himself an elephant. Like the wrestling elephants of the opening stanzas, the two creatures, beast and man, seem one.

What is said of elephants in the rest of the poem, we gather, may be applied to man. Yet, as "The Pangolin" shows, Moore knew that animal and man are not one, even though the appearance is "as if" they were. Because truth doesn't permit the identification the poet would like to make, because all man's interpretations are "as ifs," she exclaims that "we are at/much unease." Man does not have the security he would like, physical or mental; the magical attainment of "serenity" is a "masterpiece" achieved only the elephant.

The last ten stanzas investigate the nature of this achievement. The elephants are not really participants in man's activities. Ceylonese elephants are "templars of the Tooth," guardians of the tooth-relic of Buddha in Kandy. But their attitude is of "revery not reverence"—in religious ceremonies they walk in a thoughtful mood, not resisting what they cannot hope to defeat, but not giving up their independence. Yet in the naturalness of their behavior the parading elephants form what is in itself a "religious procession."

Blessed by the sacred tooth they guard, the beasts in turn bless the street they line as they watch the passage of the sacred white elephant that carries the tooth-relic itself.

Though acceding to the directions of gnatlike men, the mighty white elephant belies his skin; white, we are told, is "the color of worship and of mourning," but the elephant does not take part in human culture and is "too wise" to lament the loss of his own way of life. He is, like many of Moore's favorite creatures, "a life prisoner but reconciled." The elephant, subjected to the proddings of the mahout, is a captive who has developed the wisdom to accept with grace what he cannot prevent. Though, when first captured, he resisted till forced to curl his trunk in defeat, he has straightened his trunk now: he has learned "reason" and has "revived," has determined to live in dignity under the conditions imposed on him. The captive elephant, like man, lives in a world he did not make, did not ask for, and does not consider ideal; but he makes the best of it and, in his wisdom, sets an example for man.

Wise in his sphere as Socrates was in his, the elephant "tinctures" his "gravity" with "sweetness." He permits "man the encroacher" to make use of him; and, in accepting courteously the wishes of his conqueror, he sets an example of "brotherhood" and thus of true knowledge. He reminds us by his action of the Sanskrit verb for knowing, *bud* (related to the name "Buddha," the enlightened one). (At this point, after the first two words of what is now the next-to-last stanza, the printing of the poem in *Nevertheless* had approximately eight lines citing specific detail to show that elephants do not after all have the magical powers of Buddha—they cannot "alter their shape, bisect hairs in the dark." This passage did not further the movement of the poem, and Moore ultimately decided that its content was not necessary.)

These "knowers," the elephants, inspire the idea that they are "allied to man" and indeed that they could "change roles with" him. Reassertion of this idea indicates that we are to take the remaining six lines of the poem as applying not so much to the elephant as to man himself. "Hardship makes the soldier": fortitude, we may paraphrase, is developed through hard experience. "Teachableness," willingness to learn, then makes man into a "philosopher" who realizes that wisdom lies in being, like the elephant, modest about one's knowledge, in willingness to concede that one cannot be "sure that he knows." One necessity for serenity, that is, is willingness to live with uncertainty: to think in the "as ifs" of the sixth stanza may put us "at much unease," but it is the only possibility for the perceptive man. Who "rides on a tiger" cannot get off: he who takes the tiger as his model for behavior can never be anything other than a tiger himself. But he who relies on the elephant will develop the wisdom that brings serenity.

The elephant's survival, despite his captivity, is a product of courage; he meets the prescription for heroic behavior outlined in such poems as "What Are Years?" and "He Digesteth Harde Yron." But courage can lead to more than physical survival amid difficulties, even to more than survival of spirit. In "Elephants" Moore's speaker is saying that it can lead as well to a profound wisdom—to an acceptance, which, though guarded, is not merely passive or resistant. It can lead, that is, to that spiritual victory over "mortality" that is best named "serenity."

That "inner happiness," a quality akin to serenity, can produce a forthright craftsmanship resulting in art is demonstrated in "A Carriage from Sweden." There is in a Brooklyn museum, the poem remarks, a "country cart" from Sweden so finely made that its very presence, even though it is not at the moment on display, makes one feel at home "in this city of freckled/integrity." In its honest workmanship the cart recalls the days of Gustavus Adolphus and George Washington, days when character was not commonly "freckled." Reference to Sweden as having "once" been opposed to compromise may be a jibe at Swedish accommodation to Nazi demands during World War II, or it may be simply a suggestion that Sweden shares a general decline in integrity. In any case half a dozen stanzas exclaim over the artful construction and decoration of the carriage and the Scandinavian virtues of which it is reminiscent. These considerations lead, naturally enough, to speculation on the probable source for such spirited integrity, for a product and a people "responsive and/responsible." The answer of the last seven lines is that the source is not Sweden's topography or geology but the Swedes' combination of genuineness and imagination; it is also their ethic that values beauty, skill, and integrity. In striving to meet this stalwart ideal, the Swedes inevitably produce a work of art. The last seven lines contain a succession of *s* sounds, a series of sibilants perhaps intended to reinforce the association of Sweden with the sturdy and the skilled.

Although simplicity makes for art in "A Carriage from Sweden," there are other values than simplicity. The enchantment of complexity, of multitudinous inconsistencies, is hailed in "The Mind Is an Enchanting Thing." The paradox is that the mind enchants and is in turn enchanted. Opening remarks that the mind has the beauties of a varicolored insect wing suggest the thought that, like the kiwi or apteryx (the long-beaked, hair-feathered bird of New Zealand), the mind "walks along with its eyes on the ground": it does not need the help of sensory organs to see where it is going. It need not hear what is said, for it has the "ear" of memory; a few lines later it is the "eye" of memory—it perceives what memory wishes interpreted.

The mind is, indeed, worthy of celebration because it is "trued by regnant certainty." It, that is, has its sources in a sphere beyond this one. Thus given a fundamental stability, it can not only perceive veiled truths and remove "dejection"; it can also shimmer in an aura of iridescence and accommodate without disturbance the "inconsistencies" of a baroque composer. Being itself the height of "unconfusion," it willingly "submits" to tests of the validity of any "confusion" that may seem to appear in its understanding. It is, in short, neither a weak, unstable power easily baffled by paradox and uncertainty, nor an absolute, unchanging certitude that would, like Herod, persist in a ruthless course. Like the serene creature of "Elephants," the mind can live with and grow strong on "as ifs." It is, we gather, because of its spiritual connections both beautiful and true.

The earlier poem "In the Days of Prismatic Colour" emphasized the errors of an undue sophistication; its attitudes are reinforced, not contradicted, in "The Mind Is an Enchanting Thing" because what this poem values is not sophisticated murkiness but acceptance of the inevitable confusions of experience. The early "Melanchthon," after all, told us that there is at the core of the self a "Beautiful element of unreason." "The Mind Is an Enchanting Thing" says that awareness of the self's connection with spirit will enable one to accept "unreason" with serenity. This poem, one of Moore's best known, may be compared with the later "The Mind, Intractable Thing" that exclaims over the mind's power to call up images and present an ideal of "wordcraft" that the speaker feels she cannot achieve.

One is not, of course, to be so enchanted by his own mind that he armors himself against all feeling for others. "The Paper Nautilus" uses the military metaphor "the only fortress" to describe love. *Nevertheless* ends with "In Distrust of Merits," a poetic investigation of what Moore saw as World War II's demonstration of the need for love in human relationships. The poem incorporates considerations of the courage, armoring, guilt, and beauty that are frequent topics in Moore's work.

It has aroused critical debate because of its idealistic view of warfare and, specifically, of World War II. Somewhat like Emerson, who, a hundred years earlier, had for some time resisted involvement in the political until the fact of slavery overwhelmed him, Moore thought of herself as a nonpolitical writer until the triumphs of fascism began to disturb her. Her lack of political awareness is apparent in a letter she wrote to Bryher on 3 October 1932: "America is pestered . . . by a man named Franklin D. Roosevelt, as Germany has been with Hitler, but I think Mr. Hoover will 'win,' as our neo-Hitler would put it." Though she remained a dedicated opponent of the Roosevelts, she soon came to understand the depravities of Hitler. The papers by 1933 were full of accounts of Nazi atrocities against Jews. In the summer of that year Moore received an undated, unsigned letter from a Jewish bookseller—there is no indication whether he knew Moore personally, or simply knew of her work—recounting the interrogation under torture of himself and several other Jews in Germany in April. Moore sent the letter to the literary editor of "the New York Times—daily issue" with a note observing that "This is the subject matter we tend to spare ourselves but I think it is my duty to send it to you. . . ." Since the letter is in the Rosenbach file, it apparently was returned to her unpublished. (I find no indication of it in the *Times Index* for 1933, though all or part of it could have been incorporated in one of the several dozen stories on the situation of Jews in Germany that the *Times* published that summer and fall, or it could have appeared simply as a letter to the editor.)

Associated in her mind with the rise of Hitler was the danger of war. An entry in her notebook for 1935—dated, apparently by mistake, 2 November 1933—observes: "The one good of war is that it brings people in their helplessness to pray. It keeps people from being satisfied with an indolent peace and causes them to fight in their minds the things that make war." She does not indicate whether this observation is a quotation, or a notion that came from within herself (perhaps when she was making suggestions for one

of her brother's sermons); at any rate, the fatuousness can be excused
only on the grounds that Moore had no personal experience with
murderous savagery.

By the later 1930s Moore was pondering the place of war in
human culture. An entry for 8 March 1937 remarks that "from the
beginning life has been a struggle against death. . . . It is . . .
a struggle against death and against self—or should I say selfishness. . . ." Under 4 July 1937, she wrote "War—should be man
fighting against that in himself which is not of god." Under 9
August, she entered: "The heart is heavy as danger approaches . . . ,"
a comment she fleshed out with observations on what she saw as
the "rottenness from top to bottom" of our society. (One may suspect
again that some of these observations were set down as suggestions
to John Warner Moore.) But the insistence that war is inward
continued. On 19 September 1940 Moore wrote: "There is war
. . . war is in ourselves for only God to see. Kneeling & weeping
will not do." In June 1941 an entry begins with the phrase, given
in parentheses, that would be the title of her best-known wartime
poem, a piece that would be first published in May 1943: "(in
distrust of merits). We discard as a weed—what some could find
a use for and transform into a saviour of mankind." All of this well-
meant, idealistic view of war did not change even after Pearl Harbor
and the appearance of casualty lists in American newspapers.

"In Distrust of Merits" opens with the question whether soldiers—the Allies of World War II—have been "Strengthened" only
to achieve martial "merits." The answer is that they are fighting
not for merely military objectives but to put down the "blind" who
cannot see that enslavement of others is also enslavement of self.
Like a litany, the next lines with their prominent *o* sounds appeal
to a "star," perhaps of knowledge or truth, and to a tumultuous
ocean, perhaps the world that by its disturbance is teaching us
"depth." The exclamation "Lost at sea before they fought!" seems
less a lament for some actual event than a cry aroused by the thought
that we are "lost" because of our own deficiencies before we can
even enter a struggle for truth.

A more direct appeal calls on symbols of Judaism, Christianity,
and Ethiopia to be "joined." Ethiopia seems to represent the colored
races of mankind; and we may note that in Moore's poem, "Leonardo
da Vinci's," Ethiopia is the country of the lion that is emblematic
of Christ's resurrection. The alternatives we face are hate, that breeds

death; and love, that brings kingship and even saintliness. As the beasts of "Elephants" blessed by their worthiness the symbol they guarded, so here trust is said to breed trust.

In the third stanza the assertion becomes specific: the soldiers are fighting that "I," any one of us, may be cured of the disease "My/ Self." Their action is an atonement for our sin (a point elaborated upon in "Keeping Their World Large," where the soldiers' sacrifice is said to equal a rebirth of the spirit of Christ). In egocentrism we become self-cannibalistic: no enemy could so harm us. A man who is only physically blind can, if necessary, be escaped; but, we are reminded, Job discovered long ago that a man given the capacity to perceive who refuses to use this capacity rightly—a stubborn self—cannot be so easily evaded. All the unseeing and "arrogant" are now again admonished that trust, such trust as that accompanying love for one another, brings "power."

Therefore, the speaker declares, "We"—the plural contrasts with the "I" of self-centeredness—vow that we will never hate men no matter what skin color or creed they may have. Brotherhood of man was one of the fixed values celebrated in "The Labors of Hercules"; its difficulty of achievement again is recognized in this passage of "In Distrust of Merits" with the remark that we are "not competent" to vow it. The soldiers are the ones undergoing risk to make brotherhood effective; their heroism is what "cures me"—unless, the question occurs, "I" am "what/I can't believe in." The "I," that is, may after all be closer to the enemy than it cares to realize: it may itself harbor hatred.

Soldiers would, if struggling in anger or in hatred, be moved only by "outside" things, by merely human forces. But, when armored with patience, soldiers fight well and even in a kind of ethical beauty because, we gather, they then are responding to what Moore might have termed inside things, promptings of the spirit. As long as men act without acknowledging spirit, the world will be only a home for orphans, a desolation where peace will not come without sorrow. Yet the agonies of war will not be wasted if they "teach us how to live," to discover our spiritual sources.

The final appeal is to the "hate-hardened" heart of the self—the heart that, because it does not recognize its sources, will become rust. What this heart, this self, must see is that never was there "a war that was/not inward." The roots of war ultimately are not exterior to the individual; they lie within the self, in its failures to behave ethically. One who—like "I"—did nothing to forestall World War II, who has done nothing to rid himself of hate and to open his eyes to love, commits a treachery to the self. He must see that man, the dust of the earth, and his hatreds are only temporary; but the "Beauty" of brotherhood and the spirit is "everlasting." Soldiers can conquer only the exterior enemy. Each of us must vanquish within himself the error that is the source of the world's agonies.

The poem is in the form of a confession, almost of what in Elizabethan times was called a "complaint." Though it deals with a vast social upheaval, it is not "social poetry" but an energetic consideration of the contributions of the individual self to chaos. By this point in her career Moore, though still honoring independence of mind, was no longer advocating the kind of armoring symbolized by the cliff in "The Fish"—the aloof, almost suspicious restraint from contact with others. Yet in urging brotherhood she was still honoring individualism, for she saw brotherhood as a function of the individual heart.

Of all Moore's verse, probably only "Poetry" is better known than "In Distrust of Merits." According to A Marianne Moore Reader, when asked by Donald Hall for her opinion on the poem, she said she likes it for what she sees as the sincerity in it, but thinks it lacking in form; it is, she told him, "just a protest—disjointed, exclamatory." Nevertheless, the poem was one of the first of her works to be admitted to the college anthologies. Presumably editors found its rhetoric accessible for student readers, and liked its liberal sentiments on race relations. But the poem offended the usually enthusiastic Randall Jarrell, who is reported in the introduction to Selden Rodman's 100 Modern Poems as scorning what he saw as its message that man may be taught to live by the sufferings of war. Moore, of course, had in mind that inward war between self and temptation that had interested her since the 1930s. Yet she also had in mind, as the quotations from her writing in that era show, actual military combat. In this poem the allusions are clearly to the circumstances of World War II, not to a merely inward struggle. I must agree with Jarrell: war teaches nothing, and those of us in the European theater—and, one can be sure, those in the Pacific— fought because we were placed in a situation where there was no other recourse and because we considered that victory for the enemy would mean an eventual assault on the U.S. mainland. Moore's idealism is admirable, and the point that struggles of conscience are an inward war is, of course, valid. But the supposition that people fought and died in World War II to improve relations among races and other social groupings is ludicrous. Equally ludicrous is the assumption that a struggle of conscience can be equated with the physical brutality of warfare. Moore's fondness for taking ideas and circumstances from her reading led her astray here: the press and politicians trumpeted the ideals of the Atlantic Charter, but soldiers fought for what they considered real objectives.

The Self Reviewed

The 1981 *Complete Poems* next prints, under the heading "Collected Later (1951)," nine poems that had appeared in magazines between publication of *Nevertheless* (1944) and of *Collected* Poems (1951). The first five of these nine consider qualities the individual should have, the stance he should maintain in the universe in which he finds himself, and particularly how he may achieve the stability amid confusion that was honored in "The Mind Is an Enchanting Thing." In "A Face" the speaker, looking in a mirror, not only sees no sign of various unpleasant character traits but also sees no indication of what her real nature might be. This inability to decipher self is perhaps "no real impasse"; yet it angers the person who considers how simple the requirements for good character are: could there not be detected, she exclaims, those qualities of "ardor" and curiosity that "are all one needs to be!" The unusual grammar of this clause is intended to suggest that the desired qualities are not mere coatings or appendages but integral to the self. In contrast to the blankness the speaker sees is the memory of a few faces that remain "a delight," faces that, we deduce, showed their owners' possession of the admired qualities. The exclamatory tone of some lines and a mention of "desperation" do not make this bitter or sarcastic self-depreciation; rather, the effect is of ironic humor. Is there any among us who has not in candid moments been distressed by the revelations of the mirror?

Although the mirror arouses one kind of meditation on perfections, another kind is suggested by thought of the beings whose nature is the subject of "By Disposition of Angels." The poem opens with hypotheses about them, asking for explanation of their supposed function as messengers, suggesting that they may represent a "steadfastness" made clear by its contrast with the mystery surrounding it, and asking if they may not best be "heard" by an auditor who is perhaps at some remove from them. Angels are "unparticularities," perhaps creatures not confined to a self. They are indeed characterized by a "steadiness" heightened by its inaccessibility, just as the apparent brightness of a star is increased in a dark sky.

The angel is like a star, a fir, or speech that is indifferent to a human observer: thus the mysterious is comparable only to and is explained only by other mysteries. Yet this, we gather, makes the angel only the more interesting; "live and elate," it exists in an incomparability that obviates any "need" on our part either to draw analogies between it and people we know or to make judgments of it. It is a perfect or an ideal being that says by its existence all that need be said. We may speculate that it represents the ideal poem, and that it is to be associated with the independent behavior Moore admired. But the poem fittingly gives no obvious clues for interpretations.

Integrity obviously is a chief quality of angels, but that it is a quality we humans have yet to achieve is made apparent in "The Icosasphere," a poem inspired, as the notes explain, by accounts of an engineer's successful development of an economical method for certain utilizations of steel by study of a twenty-faced sphere. Integration of creature and function is demonstrated in the world of nature, the first stanza tells us: nesting in the "merged green density," the unified world of flora, birds unconsciously accomplish mathematical regularities that are "feats of rare efficiency." But man, lacking the perfected adjustment of animal life, displays such horrifying behavior as that found in the selfish competition of thousands of people for an inheritance to which few had a just claim. Yet man also is capable of developing the admirable icosahedron. The men who could design that might well be asked to tell us, the poem concludes, how the ancient Egyptians raised their tall granite slabs without machinery. We may take this as a wish that all of us might more easily accomplish integration of desire and action. As in "Rigorists," the approach in "The Icosasphere" is similar to that of light verse. Both poems handle with a certain playfulness a subject that seems to have no profundity. But in both Moore used presentation of her subject as a key to open the door to a consideration of ethics.

What kind of armor would help retain wholeness of being? In "His Shield" the recommendation is humility. The poem deals with the defenses of the fabled Presbyter John. This figure, more often called by the shortened title "Prester John," was a Christian leader vaguely located in Asia or Africa. He was believed to wear a garment of salamander's skin; the poem takes advantage of this detail to make purposeful allusions to the legendary ability of the salamander to survive unscathed in the midst of fires and to the related belief that asbestos was made of salamander skin.

"Everything," the opening stanza comments, "is battle-dressed." An obvious instance of this state is the porcupine; rather elaborate punning and citation allude to the Latin etymology of his name (*porcus*, pig, and *spina*, spine) and to such similar-appearing creatures as the echidna and the European hedgehog who are sometimes mistakenly identified with him. The thorny rhythm of the lines is meant to match their prickly subject matter. But a spiny coat— what because of the etymology of "porcupine" may be called "pig fur"—is not adequate for the speaker of the poem. He will prefer to shield himself in salamander skin; for thus he, like Prester John, will be able to endure the flames of life, indeed, to be a "firebrand," and to avoid drowning: he will be armored against all vicissitudes.

Yet the real shield of Prester John was not physical. His country, characterized by gusto without greed, had gold and rubies enough to make it wealthy, but it remained "unpompous." And Prester John himself, salamander-like, was so shielded against the fires of greed that he styled himself "but presbyter," not pope or bishop. Thus "His shield/was his humility": by refraining from boasting and pomp, he was able to avoid inciting invasion of his realm. Dressed without excess and accompanied only by the retinue customary for a man of moderate tastes, he was nevertheless safer than an armored knight because—like the man in "The Hero"—he had the "power" of remaining not overly concerned about his possessions; he would not let greed or pride force him to give up his freedom in a miserly fear for them.

The lines are yet another of Moore's insistences on the paradox that what she called "captivity"—the imposition of self-discipline— paradoxically breeds freedom; and they recall also the connection of peace, plenty, and wisdom asserted in "Smooth Gnarled Crape Myrtle." The concluding advice quite logically is that one should find whatever method of cloaking best defends him; but, above all, one should, like Prester John, avoid the pride that tempts the conqueror: "be/dull," not "envied." And one should not equip himself with a "measuring-rod"—make invidious comparisons of his wealth and status with those of others.

The best defense for the individual is humility, a willingness to sacrifice pride; and that this quality may be the best defense for all men in this "sick" world is suggested in " 'Keeping Their World Large.' " This poem is a counterpart to "In Distrust of Merits," which warned that egocentrism is a major cause of error and war. The soldiers who fight for a "large" world are combatting the smallness of the self narrowed by pride and greed. The poet remarks in " 'Keeping Their World Large' " that she would like to see the Italy of arts and crafts, of wisdom and angels, the homeland for various individuals who probably are residents of her own Brooklyn. She would like to see it "this Christmas Day" in "this Christmas year." We may note that the poem was inspired in part by a quotation printed in the *New York Times* in the summer of 1944 (her notes to the poem say 7 June, but the actual date was 21 August), and that it appeared in the Autumn 1944 issue of a magazine. The allusion to Christmas thus is figurative: the time is that of a Christmas, regardless of the calendar, because the poem celebrates a rebirth of what Moore regarded as Christian sacrifice and atonement.

Thought of seeing a peaceful, eternal Italy in 1944 brings to mind other paradoxical things the poet would like to find: for example, a silent piano and a "heart that can act against itself." Mention of such a heart brings up in turn the memory of Allied soldiers dying in Italy—dying in a brave willingness to match the sacrifices of Christ and of the apostles; they are willing even to die in vain if, as we can be sure Moore doubted, Christ and his followers died in vain. Against "this way" of winning—victory by sacrifice— all hearts cried out; yet the soldiers, Christlike, continue. Christ and dead soldiers remind the poet of a military cemetery with its rows of white crosses. These dead are to be seen as sacrificial offerings for the rest of us. Their spirits and their bodies, sacrificed to shield us against the "enemy"—both, we may assume, the would-be conqueror and the inward errors of self—were and remain our "shield." Their nobility should inspire us to struggle against the "fat living and self-pity" that are our less physically dangerous but nevertheless threatening enemies. Meanwhile, the poem closes, may the forthright sun shine upon "this sick scene," the whole world where war and error dominate. The poem "Leonardo da Vinci's" shows that Moore used the sun as a symbol of resurrection. The soldiers' sacrifice represents a rebirth of the Christ spirit, a "Christmas" we should attempt to bring about in our lives.

Omission of several words and some whole lines, and revisions in line breaks, make the 1981 version simpler and clearer than the *Collected Poems* printing. Omission of some verbs and subjects suggests an appropriate bit of hysteria in the speaker. Even as revised, however, the poem suggests a nobility of self-sacrifice that is remote from the reality of the Italian campaign, the bloodiest of American battlefields in World War II. The piece does demonstrate that in her middle period Moore had come to take a specifically Christian view of the nature of spirit.

The high idealism of ultimate sacrifice is not demanded in normal human experience. The last four poems return, therefore, to consideration of choices most of us may expect to be confronted with. "Efforts of Affection" remarks upon the point that love demands nourishment, that it does not come full-blown from some heavenly garden. The opening lines cite various examples of disparity—the Jubal and Jabal of Genesis who, though brothers having similar names, supposedly founded quite different lineages; Shakespeare's mention of hay that has no equal; the astonishing yet commonly experienced stubborn individualism of lovers. After viewing such oppositions, the poem comments "how welcome" it is to see the firm "integration" afforded by "unself-righteousness."

Taking another tack, the poem reflects upon the modest proclamation of a lover that he is not a saint, and it exclaims that his humility shows him to be indeed in the grip of a "Sainted obsession." The idea of attraction and of a protesting lover leads to the remark that the bleeding-heart is more attractive than perfume, whereas the elephant's-ear plant does not attempt to disguise what it is. Although both plants have selfish aims, the one is deceptive; the other, forthright. The world affords, in short, examples of disparities and deceptions but also of honesties. These contrasting possibilities may be observed in love; it, like the sun, can heal or can spoil.

Thus man lives in a situation that offers diverse choices. "Wholeness"—an "integration" including about the same qualities as those found in "wholesomeness"—is best understood not as an absolute but as the result of "efforts of affection." Spiritual unification depends, we deduce, not on attainment of an ideal but upon willingness to strive toward one. Such effort will achieve an integration that is "too tough for infraction." Variations in the style of passages in the poem reinforce the idea of diversity. The first two lines and the next-to-last stanza use a quick tempo and a diction of common words to give information and to make secondary assertions. The second and the last stanzas employ a Latinate diction, slowing the pace to convey their somewhat sentencious content. One result is an alternation of playful and serious tones to suggest that the speaker is thoughtful and reasonable, that she has a restraint in assertion because of an ironic realization that wisdom on the nature of "wholeness" has not yet been attained.

Love requires, of course, a certain aggression, an attachment of the self to someone else. That the self should be proffered only with restraint is asserted in "Voracities and Verities Sometimes Are Interacting." The poet remarks that she doesn't like diamonds, preferring the "unobtrusiveness" of emeralds. Even gratitude can at times be annoyingly intrusive. Her preference is for the unflamboyant, the Prester John of "His Shield." Thus poets, for example, should not be immodestly aggressive in their praises and declarations; other creatures, after all, have accomplishments—the elephant can express himself, the tiger can furnish interesting subject matter. Glowing diamonds and assertive poets both obtrude; both are in a sense voracious for attention, making excessive claims on one's senses. Yet, as the title indicates, there is one area in which voracity can lead to truth. One may, the ending declares, be "pardoned" for "love undying." (The phrasing is from the sixth chapter of Ephesians, Revised Standard Version.) The lover is necessarily going to violate the tenets of restraint. But he may be forgiven, for in his aggression he will come to a more profound comprehension, to a greater verity than restraint could provide.

There is an unusual crypticism in both "Efforts of Affection" and "Voracities and Verities . . . ," a suddenness of movement and a lack of explanations comparable to the procedures in "Marriage," Moore's early, long consideration of the need for effort and the nature of aggressions in relationships of love. In "Marriage" this abruptness in expression was sometimes confusing. In the two later poems the reader must make equal leaps of imagination, but he will find that the poems provide a launching pad for him to take off from. Their quickness and brevity, indeed, seem suited to the intricacy of their content.

Reconciliation of perhaps conflicting desires for integration, love, and unobtrusiveness is a function of the quality that is the subject of "Propriety." Here the poet considers the appropriateness of Brahms's technique, represented as the imitating of such natural sounds as birdsongs and of such natural actions as the spiraling of a bird up a tree. These, having "strength at the source," produce "reticence with rigor," the strong and disciplined humility Moore admired. But propriety requires an equal amount of the artfulness "in a minor key" that the poet finds in the work of Bach, the "cheerful firmness" that may be compared with such natural phenomena as the shape of a fir tree. Propriety thus is a harmony of both owl and cat, of wisdom and serenity. It is "not a graceful sadness," a sentimental melancholy; it has "wits" and it resists with humility. The qualities typified by the work of neither Bach nor Brahms should dominate, for the comprehensions of both men are involved in propriety. And both represent a natural fastidiousness "uncursed by self-inspection," a free response to inspiration. Because of its playful tone, its delight in elements of nature, and its suitably cheerful pace, this poem exemplifies the quality it describes.

Collected Poems ended with "Armor's Undermining Modesty," stanzas appropriately presenting Moore's conclusions on the theme of strength through virtue that were prominent throughout her work. Recollection of a moth that had lit on the poet's wrist— reported in the offhand but artful manner of Robert Frost—brings to mind the intricacy and beauty of the manner in which its wings were "furred." Thought of this delicate, natural accuracy calls up by contrast the blunders of man as he invented the "mis-set" alphabet. From this it is an easy step to humorous mention of the punning motto of a business firm and to a remark upon the prevalence of "faulty etymology."

Since man is unable to deal with the precise even in his mechanical activities, it is no wonder that he and his fellows can announce that "we hate poetry" and the imagery it uses. What man cannot grasp is the indirection by which poetry pursues its goals. If poetry must be explicit, the poet remarks, let us have instead of it "diatribes" and, in place of its harps and new moons, such direct appeals to the senses as the smell of iodine and of the acorn from a cork oak. Another alternative to being tastelessly explicit might be adoption of the impersonality of a deer pictured on a sales poster.

People reject poetry because they mistakenly think it to be less precise than the matter-of-fact. What is really accurate, "more precise than precision," however, is "Illusion." Thus the knights of old, such men as the storied seekers of the Holy Grail, were garbed simply and unobtrusively in the "old Roman fashion" and not like the ornate knight of modern tale-tellers who is dressed to play a role rather than appear in natural simplicity. The knights of the Grail story, dedicated as they were to virtue, wearing no "armor gilded/or inlaid," did not let anything, not even the "self," prevent them from being of use to others. One must not, we gather, let his pride in or protectiveness toward himself, his armoring of self, prevent him from communing with others. The armor with which we are to gird ourselves is to be a spiritual one, a necessary protection from the arrows of life but not a barrier to brotherhood.

Though Mars—here perhaps in his attributes as god of iron and of fortitude—can be too zealously protective of the self, heroes do not need to shun all self-protectiveness. What they would avoid is obvious enough without their having to write an "ordinall," an exact list of every sin and folly. Thus the poet would like to "have a talk with" a hero, to learn from him something of what "excess" is, and also something of the nature of that spiritual armor that enables him to overcome barriers to virtue by "undermining" them. This armoring is a product of humility; unlike gaudy outward armorings, it is not a guise of innocence covering an inner "depravity" in taste and ethics.

One vested in a mirror-bright but modest spiritual armor should be able to live up to the vows of a Grail knight and to practice a deliberate, not merely fortuitous "continence," a term meaning avoidance of error in ethics. This ability to avoid wrong is so real that it may be found "objectified"; it exists, so to speak, in an "innocence" that is true, possessing the "altitude" given by virtue and an independence that is not hackneyed by self-gratulation or other immodesties. On the one hand, the poem concludes, is a "there" occupied by immodesty, by failures in "continence"; on the other is a "there" offering to the possessor of true humility that spiritual independence all wish to attain. Man is the creature who must make choices, "The Pangolin" said. In "Armor's Undermining Modesty" we are told that the principal alternatives for man are pride or humility. The man of goodwill, the hero, will choose to steel himself in uninsistent virtue.

Omitted: Seven Discards

In the period between publication of *Selected Poems* (1935) and *Collected Poems* (1951) Moore published in periodicals seven poems that she did not print in 1951 and did not include in later books. Four of these appeared in the middle and late 1930s. They include "Half Deity" (1935), a long poem on insects that has many fine passages; "Pigeons" (1935), a somewhat playful treatment of the homing pigeon; "See in the Midst of Fair Leaves" (1936), a contrast between the swan and angel, which represent beauty, and man who in his selfishness is often an "arrow turned inward"; and "Walking-Sticks and Paper-Weights and Water Marks" (1936), a long but unified poem using a description of a walk in the country to comment on decorum and craftsmanship. All four need minor revisions to make their intentions or their syntax clear; with such revision, all four would be worth preserving.

The other three poems appeared in the early 1950s. One of these, "We Call Them the Brave" (1951), speculates on the nature of courage. "Pretiolae" (1950), a six-line poem of forty-one words, remains cryptic despite the approximately eighty words in its accompanying notes. "Quoting an Also Private Thought" (1950) is a consideration of similarities in people's thinking and of the resulting temptation to intrude upon one another.

Chapter Four
Moralist of Affairs: Translations and Prose

The poems of Moore's early and middle decades are an accomplishment of a high order, an artistic presentation of her delight in the "confusions" of our multifarious, complex, and ultimately mysterious experiences. Her poetry brings an order to experience, but only for the moment of aesthetic comprehension: the world is too much for us, but its "enchantment" may be contemplated and in some reasonably defined area its particularities may be brought into a temporary arrangement that provides a moment's stay against the confusion the mind recognizes. Moore's abilities and accomplishment reached their height in her works of the 1920s and 1930s, and continued with little diminishment through the 1940s. Meanwhile, she was turning out the translations and prose that were another voice for her muse.

The *Fables* and Other Translations

Of course Moore's adult and poetic translation of La Fontaine's *Fables* is not "the same as" his original: it is not the word-for-word Englishing demanded of a college student. Poetry is made up not of words but of a complex of associations and rhythms; the Moore translation is, therefore, not an exercise in lexicography but a venture of thoughtful imagination.

Translation of the complete work was also hard labor. Moore began the task in 1945, after W. H. Auden had suggested her name in response to a publisher's request for a translator. The translation amounts to over three hundred pages; allowing for differences in type and in page size, this is perhaps two and a half times as much verse as there is in *Complete Poems*. In eight years of intensive labor she did the entire work four times over, in addition to making innumerable revisions of individual pieces. She told me that she worked sometimes into the night, sometimes sitting up in bed in the morning. She told Donald Hall (interview in *A Marianne Moore Reader*) of the discouragement she had to overcome when Macmillan decided not to publish the work after she had given it four years of effort, and of the relief she consequently felt when Viking Press accepted it. Her conscience as a craftsman was not yet satisfied: the entire job should be done over, she told me, because though she liked the "patterns" she was not pleased with many of the rhymes.

Moore as translator applied principles apparent in her own poetry, but she maintained the form and structure of the original. This "pattern" is subjective, however; the real form and structure to her were determined not by logical sequences of rhetoric but by inward movement to a destination. Thus she wrote in the foreword to *A Marianne Moore Reader* that "The rhythm of a translation as motion . . . should suggest the rhythm of the original." The words, she added, should be "very nearly an equivalent of the author's meaning." The "very nearly" is not an alibi for incompetence but a recognition of limitations inherent in language. To maintain the overall movement of thought, she often added to or subtracted from the content of a poem. Her aim in these alterations was not to improve La Fontaine's story or statement but to maintain its spirit while achieving reasonable compliance with the urgencies of the fable's motion and while meeting the demands of English syntax and metrics. The working principle was also that of John Ciardi, who in the prefatory note to his translation of Dante's *Purgatorio* remarked that theory concerns the poet-translator "only until he picks up his pen . . . and as soon as he lays it down." That is, as an experienced poet Moore operated subjectively: the translation was good when her poetic perceptions assured her of its rightness.

She did not rely upon her own subjectivity; indeed, she had the courage to solicit suggestions and help from a number of friends and authorities whom she thanked in her foreword. As with her frequent use of quotations in her own verse, this willingness to heed others demonstrated both a catholicity of mind and a practical self-assurance that rejected fussy insistence upon self-protectiveness. The chief of these helpers was Ezra Pound, who during much of the eight years Moore was at work on the *Fables* was an inmate of St. Elizabeth's Hospital in Washington, D.C. Moore had corresponded with Pound in the heyday of the "new" poetry; she had met him when he was in New York in 1939. Now she made several trips to Washington to confer with him on her translations. She wrote in the foreword that his practice was for her "a governing principle," that she "deduced" from his works the principles of following the "natural order of words," use of active voice, avoidance of "dead words," and use of "rhymes synonymous with gusto." According to Charles Norman's biography *Ezra Pound* (1960), Pound wrote to her after seeing some of the fables in manuscript that she should rid her work of French syntax. He also suggested that she write out the sense in English prose and then versify from that paraphrase— a method that may seem profane to the romantic and the New Critic, but that the working writer often adopts.

Moore said that it was La Fontaine's craftsmanship that first drew her to him; she told me, in a somewhat cryptic note, that her work as translator was "educative" to her "ear." But she also said that the task increased her sense of "diplomacy," and in discussing his craftsmanship (foreword to *A Marianne Moore Reader*) she moved easily into citation of "certain lessons." Though craftsmanship was on her mind—a translator, after all, is a performing artist, not primarily a composer—she could not help being aware of the content and must have been pleased by its sophistication.

She must also have been pleased by its quality of presentation, a virtue she noted and reemphasized in translating the prefatory poem to the Dauphin: for La Fontaine's explanation that the happenings and fiction of his fables "contain truths that serve as lessons," she wrote that they have "Insight confirmed by direct observation." She must have been equally pleased by the fables' freedom from the arbitrary do's and don'ts of "Puritan" tradition, the prohibitions and admonitions that have taught generations of school children to value a trinity of time, money, and work; to believe that virtue always triumphs and evil is always punished; and to accept the fantasies of a Horatio Alger (whose successes typically come, be it noted, not by observation of the moralities preached in the stories but by sheer luck). It is this arbitrary, niggling version of morality that has in the twentieth century condemned the whole notion of moralizing.

La Fontaine's fables are intended not to approve or disapprove of the world but to present it as it is. La Fontaine himself in his preface defends the fable as a device for instructing children; in this introduction he cites "The Fox and the Goat" as an example of the fable's capabilities for teaching by means of a tale whose characters appeal to a child's imagination. The story is that of a goat and a fox who, while companionably strolling, grow thirsty and leap into a well to get a drink. They then realize they have no way to get out. The crafty fox suggests that he stand on the goat's horns, a platform from which he can leap to the top. The foolish goat praises the fox's wisdom and enables his escape—only to realize that there is no way out for himself. The fox triumphantly chides him, and goes away.

This is not the kind of tale favored by sentimentalists: it expresses no pity for the goat, who has been left to starve; it allots no punishment to the fox, who has coldheartedly deserted his companion; and it promises neither the Marines, the Seventh Cavalry, nor Kind Little Boy to effect a last-minute rescue. La Fontaine does not think that grasshoppers who fiddle and goats who err ought to starve, but he recognizes that in this world such is often their fate. Like Moore's own world, La Fontaine's is one wherein peril is always lurking and wisdom calls for courageous forethought.

His emphasis is not on praise or blame; the typical fable is not a story of a contest between virtue and vice, but a contrast of proper and foolish responses to a situation. In "The Eagle, the Sow, and the Cat," for example, a cat's malicious gossip of imaginary dangers so troubles its neighbors that, in misguided attempts to protect their broods, they allow them to starve. The verse editorial of the fable's short final stanza stays with the point that the circumstances have demonstrated: false tongues can do harm. It does not bring in a punishment of the cat or otherwise expand the point beyond the limits of the event itself. We are to see one lesson, the foolishness of the eagle and the sow in failing to detect the meanness of the cat. This does not glorify wrongdoing; but neither does it make martyrs of the stupid. The lesson is that this is a world where wickedness is to be met with; instead of crying over this fact of experience, we should learn to cope with it.

La Fontaine subjects innocence itself to much examination, as in "The Wolf and the Lamb" with its moral that "Force has the best of any argument." The lesson that innocence is not a sufficient armoring against force is surely upheld by a look at the world around us. Similar practical wisdom appears in "The Vultures and the Pigeons," a story of peacemaking small birds who, in order to halt a senseless war, get big birds to agree among themselves; but the little ones are then ruined because the big birds turn on them. Common sense, that is, bids us to be alert to our own interests because action on principle may be turned against us. Another important moral is that those near the centers of power must be cautious. "The Lion Holds Audience" tells how the king lion banishes both the critical bear and the fawning monkey, letting only the reticent fox escape unpunished. The less perceptive moralist assumes that the way to get ahead in court is to flatter; but La Fontaine shows the bitter truth that the powerful are quite likely to be arbitrary in use of their strength, that the flatterer does not necessarily succeed with them, and that the best armor therefore is circumspection. In these fables La Fontaine is not a cynic attacking ideals of justice and peacemaking, nor even formulas for success. He is a realist pointing out that the ideal is by no means always achieved, that the outcome of events is not always controllable. He implies always a contrast between what is and what ought to be, but he does not write in a reforming zeal because he is sophisticated enough to assume that reform is not to be expected within his lifetime. His intent is to alert us to the ways of the world and thus instruct us in the wisdom necessary to cope with it.

Sometimes La Fontaine exhibits his own moral standards by giving contrasting treatments to two fables similar in content. "The Dairymaid and Her Milk-pot" pictures a girl who allows dreams of grand enterprises developing from the sale of her milk to cause her to skip for joy; in so doing, she lets her milk container break. La Fontaine comments wryly that we all daydream, that even he had his fantasies of being a king until reality returned to show him that, though he had a king's troubles, he did not have a king's rewards. The tale immediately following this one, "The Cure and the Corpse," has essentially the same point. But the circumstances in it are distasteful: the priest is a mercenary dolt who counts his probable takings from a rich parishioner even while participating in his funeral service. La Fontaine therefore gives him a deserved punishment: death strikes when the coffin suddenly falls on him. The milkmaid's error was petty because it consisted of mere dreaming; the priest's was serious because it was outright greed.

La Fontaine's harsh observations of the workings of the world appear cynical at times. In "The Animals Sick of the Plague" the point is that judgments depend upon whether one is weak or strong, the weak being likely candidates for condemnation.

Most of the fables exhort to avoidance of error, but occasionally La Fontaine suggests what an ideal life might include. Its essential characteristic would be the humility that leads to contentment with one's situation. Ambition and greed are synonymous. Thus the country mouse finds the city mouse's life too dangerous; the male in "The Two Doves" discovers that he should be content with his wife rather than roam the world for happiness; the mogul in "The Mogul's Dream" learns that the life leading to bliss in the hereafter will be a contemplative one that avoids cares, ambitions, and competition.

But in the fables there are enough passages making use of mirror imagery and valuing withdrawal from the world to suggest that La Fontaine was serious in advocating contemplative solitude. Yet retreat from the world is not to be fanatical or merely selfish. "The Rat Retired from the World" tells of a weary rat who, ensconced in a rich cheese, became so devoted to his gross comforts that he refused to contribute even to the defense of his city. Not his retirement but his fanaticism, his selfish concentration on his own satisfaction, is to blame for his coldness. What one should want is shown in "The Wishes," a tale of how men given three wishes find the wealth they first ask for burdensome and the poverty they return to not entirely satisfactory; only the wisdom they finally request proves worth having. A principal responsibility to La Fontaine, as to Moore, was to the self. Neither recommended life as a recluse, but both urged a moderation in desire that would leave one free to engage in the contemplation necessary if he was to know himself. Moore went a step farther, of course; in her translations seclusion is recommended not only to enable acquisition of self-knowledge but also to allow for a process of "seeking the source": she would scrutinize the self in order to understand what she was convinced are its spiritual origins.

Perhaps the chief contribution of the translation to Moore's own value system was its exemplification of the morality of the man of action. La Fontaine pictures aspects of life Moore did not write about and, except for her few years in teaching and on the *Dial,* seldom experienced directly. She wrote of self-reliant individualists, typically of the jerboa or ostrich or basilisk that survive in a man-dominated world without being part of it; her code of ethics was adequate for these solitaries. Through La Fontaine's verse she could obtain vicarious experience in a realm of "affairs," of the behavior of the powerful in politics, business, and high society. La Fontaine gives a mature presentation of the code of conduct necessary, or at least advisable, in the world where the individual self is in competition with the striving selves of other individuals. Moore did not necessarily approve of the conduct he depicts, but neither did he. And his presentation of the world as a scene of peril did not conflict with hers. The chief difference is in attitude toward mankind's future in the dark environment both poets see. La Fontaine's sophistication made him a pessimist, unlikely to believe in the possibility of significant reform. But Moore's assurance that a saving spirit exists made her an optimist; she expected that mankind, though now weak, can, with proper armoring, be triumphant.

Both poets wrote of animals; a comparison of their tactics gives insight into their craftsmanship. "I make use of animals to instruct men," La Fontaine told the Dauphin in his dedicatory verses; in the preface he remarked that fables about animals work not only to extend knowledge of animal behavior but also our understanding of ourselves because "we epitomize both the good and the bad in creatures of restricted understanding." His typical fable is a story telling a lesson, usually incorporating a direct statement of the moral. Animals enact roles that the reader knows only human beings would actually carry out; the whole point of a fable is not the fox-ness or stork-ness or lion-ness of its characters; but their resemblance to men, their representation of human qualities. La Fontaine seldom describes the animal, for what is important is not its appearance and its animal nature but its function in the story. He deliberately relies on stock characters, taking advantage of the fact that his reader will see the wolf as rapacious, the fox as sly, the lamb as innocent.

Moore's use of animals in her own verse was quite different. Her presentation was descriptive rather than narrative, and she wanted moral and other "meanings" to come from her handling of her materials rather than from the outcome of a story. Her jerboa is clearly a desert rat, not a man in animal clothing; her pangolins and basilisks and lions are equally themselves. They live and act according to their animal natures and not as men who happen to wear feathers or furs. Wishing to avoid stock reactions, she often chose to deal with exotic animals. Because she lavishes description upon her creatures, her own poetry had more color and ornament than La Fontaine's; even her translation of his work is somewhat less spare than his original because she tucked in bits of description as, for example, in "The Fox and the Crow" and in "The Frog Who Would Be an Ox." But the fable is hardly so esoteric a form that a skilled artist could not successfully operate within it; Moore as translator accepted La Fontaine's form as well as his substance.

She also attempted to match the skill of his technique in order to reproduce the dry, realistic comment that has won international acceptance of his work as a wise and shrewd presentation of human conduct. She not only often succeeded brilliantly in conveying the spirit of his work; she sometimes improved on it. The ending of "The Faithless Depository"—the story of how a merchant subdues a tricky businessman by out-tricking him—is in La Fontaine's version a musing, functional but not particularly pointed comment, translating literally as:

> When the absurd is outlandish, one does it too much honor
> In wishing to combat its error by reasoning:
> It is briefer to go it one better, without heating up the temper.

Moore writes:

> When speech forsakes sound sense, judiciousness forbears.
> Don't aspire to right wrongs or be splitting hairs:
> Best out-Herod your bore and surmount his ill will.

She quickened the pace, making the expression terse; and she introduced the notion of splitting hairs and the idea of Herod. She did not in this instance reproduce La Fontaine's world-weary casualness, but she gave what is, all the same, an apt ending for the story.

Often her terse style suitably matched La Fontaine's spareness, and she succeeded at the same time in finding poetic—not merely literal—equivalents for the spirit of his story. A literal translation of the ending of "The Two Doves" is:

> Ah! if my heart dared again to be inflamed!
> Wouldn't I feel more the charm that has given me pause?
> Have I passed the age for love?

Moore's version reads:

> Ah! might my heart take fire once more in the old way.
> Alert even now to love's spark and, elate,
> Beat fast as in a former day.

La Fontaine introduces by means of "dared" and the questioning last line a pathos that is reproduced in Moore's translation by the sentimental "old way." She often reproduced the syllable count and the rhyme scheme of La Fontaine's version. Sometimes she matched his use of other devices as well. Thus in "The Grasshopper and the Ant" she could not duplicate exactly the various repetitions of sound that he employed in the opening lines; but, she told me, she was pleased with the fact that she was able to make use of other sound repetitions suggestive of these (chose . . . chirr; chew . . . chirred . . . chant).

Moore's skill at its best is to be seen in "The Judge, the Hospitaler, and the Hermit." In this fable La Fontaine uses within the last six lines of the long first stanza the rhymes *opposer-reposer*, and *solitaire-salutaire*. She matched this with *ambition-commotion, source-course*. Her first line for the second stanza, "Don't infer that I mean that work is a curse," makes an imperative of his indirect "It is not that work doesn't have to be endured." As often, she was, in making the expression somewhat more pointed, speaking partly in her own voice; but she was also interpreting the gist of what La Fontaine's artful casualness keeps him from saying directly.

There is no need to give extended comparison of passages. What comparison reveals is not that one poet is better than the other, but that each is himself or herself. Moore as translator was faithful but not slavish. One should still read La Fontaine in the French. But the reader will find Moore's Englishing of his work to be good poetry in its own right.

Reviewers, predictably, differed in their opinions: we have few standards for assessment of translations. Though Moore thought the entire work needed rewriting, the majority of reviewers praised it; even some who doubted its worth—John Ciardi, Ramon Guthrie, Stephen Spender—found good words for aspects of it. Only two reviewers at the time wrote outright attacks. Howard Nemerov, in a joint review of the *Fables* and of Ciardi's version of Dante's *Inferno*, said neither translation is worthwhile. Mary M. Colum was the most thoroughly unfavorable, finding neither Moore's expression nor her content suited to the original. Today's writers on Moore have little to say about the *Fables*, the prevailing opinion apparently agreeing with Helen Vendler's view that "Not a great deal should be claimed for them," that they are "finally not satisfying as poems by Moore."[1]

To give the poet herself the last word, we may note that she told
Lewis Nichols of the *New York Times* that her favorites were "The
Dog Who Dropped Substance for Shadow" and "Bitch and Friend"
(her views evidently changed: neither of these is among the five she
chose to reprint in the 1967 version of *Complete Poems*). She also told
Nichols that she was unhappy with "Middle Age and Two Possible
Wives," "The Two Parrots, the King and His Son," and "The Kite,
the King, and the Hunter."

The *Fables* were Moore's major work as a translator. Aided by
Elizabeth Mayer, she had earlier published *Rock Crystal* (1945), a
translation of a Christmas story from Adalbert Stifter's *Bunte Steine*.
This work is perhaps best described as an exercise in style. It tells
of two children who lose their way in the Alps on Christmas Eve
but are found in the bright sunrise of morning, the implication
being that they have been saved by a vision. Moore's retelling is
polished but cold. The children never become interesting as people,
and the writing is too Latinate in diction and too intricate in syntax
for the general reader.

In 1962 Moore published a lively four-act dramatic version of
The Absentee, Maria Edgeworth's novel of manners. Edgeworth had
originally written the story as a play, but rewrote it as a prose tale
when Richard Brinsley Sheridan turned it down. The original stage
version has disappeared; Moore's work, therefore, is a restoration.
In a typically economical foreword, she defends it against possible
accusations that it is obsolete by citing famous authors—Ruskin,
Scott, Macaulay—who have praised it and by asserting that there
are "counterparts everywhere" to its characters. The questions she
suggests the critic might ask indicate her interest in both craftsmanship and lessoning: "Does it hold attention? Does any of it
apply?" In 1963 Moore published a "retelling" of three of Charles
Perrault's tales, "Puss in Boots," "The Sleeping Beauty," and "Cinderella." As with the *Fables,* she employed early manuscripts and
worked with the advice of a number of editors and professors.

Prose: Varieties of Style

Though the total of her reviews, essays, and other works preserved
in *Complete Prose* (1986) comes to 689 pages, Moore did not write
a unified work of sizable length in prose. She published a selection
of her essays and reviews in *Predilections* (1955). Additional pieces

appeared in *A Marianne Moore Reader* (1961); and two essays appeared
as the slim book *Idiosyncrasy and Technique* (1958). *Complete Prose*
contains all the prose that she published. The Rosenbach Collection
holds much of her extensive correspondence, as well as reading
diaries that often have comments similar to those she printed. More
letters are in the Beinecke Library. Moore used prose for literary
comment and for occasional presentation of opinions and impressions
on other topics. She sought in both her own prose and that of others
the accuracy of perception and the "gusto" and "idiosyncrasy" in
expression that she sought in verse. Her prose, that is, is another
channel for expression of the impulses toward imaginative comprehension that fueled her verse writing.

Somewhat like the essays of Emerson and Thoreau, the pieces in
Complete Prose are studded with phrasings that at first glance seem
to outweigh in importance any overall statement. Thus in a 1929
review of *Mist,* a novel by Miguel de Unamuno, she singled out for
quotation the description of a woman's hand as "a hand made, not
for grasping, but only for perching, like the foot of a dove—upon
the shoulder of her husband." She ended the brief notice with a
sentence containing quotations that, as often in her verse, seem to
be observations of her own that she chose to quote both in order to
highlight them and to preserve reticence by distancing herself from
them a bit: " 'Confusionist, indefinitionist' art of this kind is like
the piano, of no service, merely serving 'to fill the fireside with
harmony and keep it from being an ash-pit.' " And, as in her verse,
her observations are sometimes so compact that one must read with
care. They are worth the effort because their terse expression holds
directly to the point: thus, in a review of *Letters of Emily Dickinson,*
she notes that the editor, Mabel Loomis Todd, had exercised a
reticence that included "care lest philistine interest in what is fine
be injudiciously taxed."

She told me, and many others over four or more decades, that
she preferred not to make adverse comments on the writing of others.
But she nevertheless let herself be critical. She was somewhat amusedly
tart in an observation in "The Hawk and the Butterfly" (a 1934
essay on Yeats): "We are warned by Mr. Yeats that in our speaking
of his doctrines we may be talking about what no longer exists; but
the poems exist and should he now ignore the tinge on them of
disclaimed speculation he nevertheless must pardon our thinking
about what he formerly may have thought." When she wished to,

she could be devastating. In a 1937 review of *How Writers Write*, edited by Nellie S. Tillett, she wrote that William Ellery Leonard "defeats his purpose as though bewitched"; in the same review she remarked that "One wishes that Ellen Glasgow's sanity, moral courage, and contagious spontaneity, were not marred by inadvertent triviality."

But, like her Transcendental predecessors, she made her essays more than mere collections of idiosyncratically phrased opinions. "Feeling and Precision," for example, begins with the observation that the deepest feeling is likely to be inarticulate, and that if it is articulate it "is likely to seem overcondensed," arousing resistance to the author "as being enigmatic or disobliging or arrogant". The reticence, the humility of statement that she so often speaks of in verse as well as in prose, arises, it appears, from conviction that direct statement is not only economical but also precise: one should present the thing as it is, leaving explanation to those who want it. After stating preferences in sentence form, she turns to several paragraphs of observations on precision. As ever, she makes her presentation an amalgam of her own observations and shrewdly chosen quotations that enable her to get her point across without seeming to assert it directly. One cannot resist quoting the passage she chooses from Daniel (10: 9–10) and her comment on it: " 'Then was I in a deep sleep on my face, and my face toward the ground. And, behold, an hand touched me, which set me upon my knees and upon the palms of my hands. And I stood trembling.' Think what *we* might have done with the problem if we had been asked to describe how someone was wakened and, gradually turning over, got up off the ground."

Two paragraphs on the deficiencies of "artificial art" lead to a set of paragraphs on feeling, again given as an apparently rambling set of observations, frequently using quotation, yet coming to the relation of rhyme and feeling and thus to observations on jargon and diction. These conclude with a quotation from Jacques Maritain supporting Moore's insistence that "belief is stronger even than the will to survive." This brings on the concluding remark that art is an expression of needs, is "feeling, modified by the writer's moral and technical insights." What Moore set down is a marvelous presentation of the unbreakable unity of thought and writing, of the ways that precision and feeling support, both originate and express, one's being. The works in *Complete Prose* show that she had many arrows in her quill: she could lean even more heavily on quotation, as in the essay "Henry James as a Characteristic American"; she could be economical and efficient, as in the brief statement "Brooklyn from Clinton Hill"; she could be playful, admiring, sad, or disapproving; notably, she could, as in her 121 "Briefer Mention" pieces for the *Dial,* compress exact statement and complex opinion into a paragraph. We must look forward to publication of selections from her reading diaries and her correspondence. Her prose exemplifies, again, the qualities of idiosyncrasy and technique, the "gusto" that she desired in poetry.

Chapter Five
Reaffirmations:
Late Period Poems

Publication in 1961 of *A Marianne Moore Reader* indicated the poet's arrival as a celebrity and as a writer known to a wider public than critics and her fellow modernists. The *Reader* gives a sampling of her essays and reviews, twenty-three pieces from *Collected Poems* and twenty-four from *Fables*, an interview with Donald Hall, all of *Like a Bulwark* (1956) and *O to Be a Dragon* (1959), and five "other poems," four of them recent and one, "Sun," a reprinting of a poem that first appeared in 1916. The prose includes "The Ford Correspondence" (1956–57), letters between Moore and a Ford representative concerning the naming of a new model. Moore made a number of imaginative suggestions, but the company eventually settled for the Ford family name Edsel. The correspondence is amusing in itself, and the fact that the Edsel failed to attract the public seems a fate the company deserved for rejecting Moore's proposals. Fame brought its usual penalties, however. Moore was besieged for the rest of her life with requests from authors of term papers and dissertations, amateur poets, and other writers.

Like a Bulwark

The eleven poems published in 1956 under the title *Like a Bulwark* had all previously appeared in magazines; in acknowledging permission to reprint them, Moore remarked that "Tom Fool" and "The Staff of Aesculapius" were "much improved" by magazine editors—an acknowledgment few poets would have the courage to print.

The 1981 printing opens with "Like a Bulwark," a poem that first appeared as "At Rest in the Blast" and then as "Bulwarked Against Fate." The "object" dealt with is the poet herself, who is conceived of as one of those armored, self-sufficient creatures of whom Moore was fond. The poem opens in the third person, with an abrupt one-word sentence ("Affirmed") giving an appropriately hard, almost staccato tone to the assertion that the object is disciplined by what gives it value. By the third line, the poem is in the second person, directly addressing its object: "you," it says, "take the blame and are inviolate." The connective is "and," not "yet," for the poet wants to present two direct assertions. This creature—the poet's own spirit—thus is self-sacrificing and innocent. But it is also deservedly proud. Though "tempest-tossed," it is not "abased"; it is made compact by the "blast" that assaults it until it becomes fortified, "a bulwark against fate." It is, indeed, compressed to the density of lead.

The closing lines probably are intended as a pun on this experience, the salutary effects of compression reminding the poet of bullets fired in military salute, and this in turn reminding her of the "bulwark" or fortress of spirit that is, in its way, as worthy of formal honors as a military post. The poem is another celebration of the armored spirit; it might also be read as a comment upon poetic style, an assertion of the virtues of compression. It is an example of the highly compact work that Moore thought was firmest and had the best chance of surviving. The poem is much revised from the magazine version.

From the thoughts of Old Glory that closed "Like a Bulwark" it is an easy move to "Apparition of Splendor" which presents the porcupine as an example of a bulwark. Here what is praised, however, is the creature's "symmetry" with nature. The poem opens with allusions to an animal seemingly "miraculous" that was pictured by Dürer, allusions hinting at spiritual and aesthetic status for the porcupine. The third stanza remarks factually that the porcupine has "never shot a quill"; in thus correcting a persistent folk belief, the poem gains an air of authenticity that is supported by the specific descriptions of the animal's barbs that are intermingled in stanzas 4 and 5 with further allusions to fictional and fairy-tale porcupines.

Through the first five stanzas we are presented with the half-literal, half-legendary creature that is somehow in harmony with the forest surrounding it. Belief in the existence of such harmony seems to suggest that the forest, the world itself, shares some of the "joyous fantasy" the poem delights in. The last stanza then hails the porcupine for his steadfastness and peacefulness; the editorializing of the stanza grows directly, detail by detail, from the picture already given. If the animal is in part the "apparition" mentioned in the title, it is one of "splendor" because it is a "resister" to the oppressive and the insistent: it is, indeed, like a bulwark. The paradox that both the white and the dark are associated with truthfulness leads to assertion of the value of truthfulness in "Then the Ermine:," a poem treating its subject with an intense seriousness that is not betrayed by the ironic humor that infuses it. Truthfulness is the opening concern, the title and first line alluding to the idealism of Clitophon, son of Kalander in Sir Philip Sidney's *Arcadia*. The poet tells us that she too has idealism, wanting to be regarded as trustworthy in her assertion that she saw a bat abroad in the daytime. In the bat's insecure but courageous persistence in its aims, it reminded her not of heavy-handed "bravado" but of a duke's motto, "I spurn to change or to take fright." This causes her to reflect that she too does not change and is not "craven"—though she cannot say for sure that it would always be difficult to frighten her. The air of thoughtful reflection, of conversational intimacy with the reader, seems intended to carry him along into the more compressed reflections in the last four stanzas. Thought of the bat's "wavering" flight—like that of a jack-in-the-green, the man concealed in boughs who took part in May Day rites—leads to the possibility of failure.

If she does not achieve her aims, she remarks in the fifth stanza, the physiography of Johann Lavater will have "another admirer." Lavater was a Swiss versifier and pastor whose best-known work is a study of physiognomy. Both physiography, the description of nature and natural objects, and physiognomy, the study of human appearances, were of interest to Moore herself; her speaker seems to be remarking that if she fails in her own presentations she will admire all the more intensely the skill Lavater demonstrated. His art, it appears, lay particularly in his ability to make the obscure lucid, a skill "now a novelty," the speaker asserts.

Yet, since "nothing's certain," we should allow others the expression of changeability we may not desire in ourselves. A palisandre settee—one decorated with human, animal, and plant figures— may properly show in one and the same scene a crow "in full dress" and a shepherdess, representatives of utter naturalness and of highly artificial dignity. Such obvious expression is acceptable; however, the "wavering" bat and the poet who fears that she may fail have their potential also. The "foiled explosiveness" they represent prophesies action to come that may give success to their efforts though being, paradoxically, "a concealer." Like the bulwark and the armored animals that Moore admired, concealed possibility has power, here a power of "implosion," of bursting inward like the violets depicted by Dürer. The poem closes with the line "even darker," seemingly an allusion to color symbolism in which the violet stands for love of truth. Such color symbolism also perhaps accounts for description of the crow as "ebony violet" and for mention of a shepherdess (who is possibly from Ionia, a province named for the violet). The title seems to indicate a continuation, taking up the ermine which is also a symbol of truth.

Ideal behavior is not quiescent nor dull, but spirited; this is evident in the next two poems, "Tom Fool at Jamaica" and "The Web One Weaves of Italy." Tom Fool was a race horse, much praised by a *New York Times* sportswriter referred to in Moore's notes. Her speaker treats the horse, like the porcupine, as an "apparition of splendor"; but emphasis now is upon the belief that excellence of performance indicates the presence of such underlying moral qualities as persistence in the face of difficulty and resolution to perform to the best of one's ability—qualities Jonah exhibited in his famous voyage. Though purposeful, Jonah did not pretend to infallibility; indeed, instead of working for impossible perfection, it would be better to imitate the schoolboy who, too young to be limited by realism, showed a man on a mule blocked by a snail. To feel with ardor, as the boy did, this is "submerged magnificence," and this is the quality of Tom Fool.

This consideration of possibility within the improbable may be owing to Moore's own mixed feelings, for her notes say that, though attracted to the horse by the sportswriter's description, she was bothered by its connection with gambling. In any case, the speaker moves on with comments on the horse, citing a remark that Tom Fool finds the resolution to make the extra spurt that is the "mark of a champion." A bit of playfulness in alluding to a picture of Tom Fool printed on April Fool's Day serves to keep the presentation from overwhelming seriousness, as does the familiar reference to a racetrack announcer as "Signor" rather than "Mr." Capossela (he is mentioned deliberately; for, as the poem remarks, he told an interviewer that he does not bet on horse races). The fourth stanza then is a climax: what a moralist can find to admire, after all, is some of the color and seeming artistry of a race scene; forgetting the purpose for a moment, one can enjoy the colors, rhythms, and harmonies. Half-humorously, the poet brings the stanza up short with the remark "well—this is a rhapsody." We gather that extended rhapsodizing would be out of place because the purpose of horse racing cannot be excluded from any complete picture. Rather than continue with the racing scene, she turns in the last stanza to consideration of other kinds of "champions." Fittingly she alludes to noted performers of jazz, another quasi-art wherein style is more important than substance. A couple of quick references to racetrack sights leads to the ending, "But Tom Fool. . . ." The inconclusiveness suggests that complete description of the horse's qualities is impossible. Illustrative of Moore's confidence in her ability to include the humorous, almost ludicrous, without destroying a poem is her reference in the last two lines to the sight of "a monkey/on a greyhound"—an example of racing, to be sure, but hardly one to please a horse-race fan. Moore's speaker, of course, is suggesting slyly that what is important is the moral excellence the poet saw in aesthetic appeals and strength of character, not degrees of status among gambling enterprises.

That spectacle may be nonintellectual but not necessarily mindless is suggested in "The Web One Weaves of Italy." So much goes on in Italy, the poet remarks, that the visitor hardly knows where to turn. What goes on is a list of tourist activities including a crossbow tournament, peach fairs, and mule shows. But these are regarded here as a "modern *mythological/esopica,*" a series of activities having, like Aesop's fables themselves, moral implications despite—perhaps even because of—their qualities as "nonchalances of the mind." What happens is "quite different" from the formal education given at a Sorbonne; yet it is "not entirely" unlike intellectual enterprise, for in its Aesop-like suggestiveness it is something "more than . . . spectacle." The poem ends with the assertion that "Because the heart is in it all is well." It is the presence of "the heart," we gather, that enables seemingly trivial activities to share some of the qualities of wisdom or knowledge presumably imparted by a university: the heart and the head, though different, are not entirely separate.

The remaining six poems in the volume are occasional pieces, some commissioned by editors for holiday issues of magazines, others celebrating or inspired by an experience. "The Staff of Aesculapius" appeared first in *What's New*, a publication of the Abbott Laboratories. It celebrates the medical researcher for his persistence, his abandonment of "vague speculation," and his willingness to adopt temporary measures while working diligently for permanent ones. Lines 2, 3, and 4 of the fourth stanza incorporate an expression from a prose report ("Selective injury to cancer/cells without injury to/ normal ones . . .") at the cost of a slight sag in the rhythm, but they preserve the exactness in both tone and statement of the original with a clarity superior to the somewhat artificially poetic syntax used in the fifth stanza to present substance that is equally factual. Yet this stanza serves its purpose as climax, for in Moore's deliberately offhand way it incorporates the remark that as a result of the new surgical technique "what/was inert becomes living." This technique and the scientific medicine it represents are, so the last stanza's question implies, like the marvelous rod of Aesculapius. The rod with its entwined snake is a symbol of the renewal medicine gives to man. The poem, by exploring exact details of medical activity, has found an exemplification of the persistence Moore valued.

Chance sight of an impressive tree probably gave rise to "The Sycamore," a poem remarking that there is "grace" in the small as well as in the large. The sycamore, apparently seen in late autumn, appeared an "albino giraffe" that might arouse the envy of either the varicolored or the pure white. The creatures mentioned as perhaps being stirred to envy are much smaller than a tree, and the contrast of their smallness with its grandeur brings on the observation that "there's more than just one kind of grace." There is, for instance, the grace of such small things as flowers and that of the miniature paintings produced by camel-hair brushes. Worthy of preservation by a noted miniaturist, the poem concludes, was "a little dry/thing from the grass"—probably an insect—seen in a field near the great tree; it seemed to feel humble as a mouse before a palace. Seeing grace in both the large and the little, Moore seems in this poem to honor the small and humble.

Another of several Christmas poems by Moore is "Rosemary," which honors Christ's birth by exploring legendary symbolisms of the rosemary plant. Beauty and her son—Venus and Love, "to speak plainly," we are told—braid a festive garland of rosemary at Christmas. Though the poem alludes to Greek mythology, its theme is Christian, a point indicated by the etymological comment that the plant was "not always rosemary." (The English name comes from the Latin *Ros marinus,* "dew of the sea"; in classic times rosemary was associated with Venus as a fellow child of the ocean, and thus with Venus's son Love. *Ros marinus* at first was anglicized to rose-marine, and was altered to its present form under the influence of the words "rose" and "Mary.")

This etymology, and the facts that the Virgin Mary is often referred to by such terms as Star of the Sea and is frequently symbolized by a rose, all have significance. Before the plant's association with the Holy Family, it was something other than rosemary, the poem suggests; the stanza reports the Spanish legend, explained in the notes, that the rosemary originally had a white flower but, as the herb of memory, has remained blue since Mary spread her robe on a clump of it during the flight into Egypt. Yet, the poem cautions, we are to remember this is an actual flower, "not too legendary" to be real in its "pungency." The poem closes with a final remark on the storied and real attributes of the rosemary, both helping to make it "in reality/a kind of Christmas-tree." The plant's "reality," like that of the porcupine in "Apparition of Splendor," is not that of the realist who values only appearances: it is rather a combination of the spiritual and the sensory.

If the whole of reality includes both the natural and an extra-natural, it follows that a means of expressing this must itself succeed in yoking the physical and the spiritual, perhaps in expressing the one through the other. This idea is advanced in "Style," a poem that seems a commentary not only on art but upon all behavior. In choosing presentation of and commentary on Spanish and Basque performers as a device for expressing this idea, Moore seemed to imply need for passion within discipline.

The poem opens with the assertion that style "revives"—apparently it is all too frequently somnolent—in the dancing of Vicente Escudero, whose control and precision extend even to placement of his hat. We in the United States had our own careful performer in Dick Button, the skating champion; but to suggest that we are related to the performers of southwestern Europe, Moore's speaker also remarks on Etchebaster, the Basque athlete who won an American tennis championship. Mention of Etchebaster prompts remarks upon Soledad, the Spanish woman dancer who performed in the United States in 1950 and 1951. A pun on her name—"aloneness"—reinforces the declaration that Soledad's black garb does not indicate sadness; a series of similes then indicates half a dozen ways one might attempt to describe the precise figures she performed. So admirable, indeed, are her competencies that she may be forgiven her former career as a bullfighter—a concession one realizes Moore would not easily make. The fourth stanza quickly cites an individual characteristic or two for Etchebaster, Vicente Escudero, and Rosario Escudero. Each of these men had his own mode of behavior or favorite hallmark; in each case it was an inseparable part of his style, of the fitting way of expression he had found for himself.

Having explored the possibilities of a variety of comparisons that might enable one to explain the essence of style, the poet now pretends to surrender: the effort ends in defeat, for "There is no suitable simile." At least, however, we gather that style, a manner of expression that is perfectly suited to substance, will join two or more apparently distinct entities. Fitting expression, the poem concludes, is like a conjoinment of the "arcs of seeds" in a banana by a musician; or it may be said to be like a painter's depiction of the face of a musician. The poem ends not with a bit of syllogistic logic but with an exclamatory repetition of the names of the four performers who are its principal characters. This exclamation seems to imply that better than attempting to describe the indescribable is a simple citation of examples.

The paradox that a large-scale opera could appear on an ordinary television screen is explored with some of Moore's humor but with her usual seriousness of purpose in "Logic and 'The Magic Flute,' " written after seeing a color telecast in 1956 of the opera named in the title. Several remarks and puns refer to seashells, which are sometimes associated with Venus, the goddess of love who was born from the ocean; allusions are also made to the wentletrap, an elegant shell once much valued by collectors because of its spiral shape. This shape bears some resemblance to a spiral staircase, a fact indicated in the etymology of its name, and one important enough to cause Moore to include an illustration of the shell in her notes to the poem.

The opera, we are told, seems to carry her "Up winding stair" as though she were lost in a strange theater. The action appeared on a small screen near a magazine rack in the "abalonean gloom" of a darkened living room, and it was accompanied by the "intrusive hum" of the television set's workings; these impressions seemed to fill the room. But the scene then carried the viewers abruptly out of doors, where it seemed that "a demon" roared the question whether one might ever find love. That the "demon" cried "down" stairs of marble perhaps indicates that he had pressed on ahead in a search that also engaged the speaker of the poem; that the stairs were marble suggests an appropriate coldness, and perhaps also is an indirect allusion to the seashell motif. At any rate, the answer to the query is "simple." We need only "Banish sloth," the tyrant that pretends to fetter us, to keep us from active recognition and acceptance of the "Trapper Love" that, itself a "magic sleuth," will surely find us if we are open to its discovery. "Illogically" but surely, love has by means of the music woven the realization that "logic can't unweave," the understanding that to have love we need not compete, need not fight.

From love the concern moves to beatitude in "Blessed Is the Man," a poem of interest not only for its presentation of certain of Moore's own principles but also for its differences from the ideas and techniques of the Beat movement then (1956) in vogue. True beatitude, Moore held, comes from practice of traditional but far from universally honored values; one arrives at it not by defiance nor by a process of becoming a martyr within his society, but by holding himself aloof. The opening stanza puts together a biblical allusion, a phrase from an attack on President Eisenhower, and a book reviewer's quotation from Lincoln to declare that the man is blessed who does not criticize, who is not given to intemperance and alibis, and who stands firmly for what he thinks is right.

The second stanza alludes to a self-portrait by Giorgione; the fact that his work is usually unsigned serves to caution the reader that the blessed man, though firm in principle, is not a victim of "egomania." Diversity with tolerance makes a "fort," a bulwark that will "armor" the blessed man as he makes decisions on the basis of aptness to a situation, to a principle, and to public interest. This man, a Ulysses in leadership, will find that his fellows of this age "are now political"—as in the La Fontaine tale quoted in stanzas 4 and 5, they have become brutes. Examples are "Brazen authors" who coat the conscience to resist questions raised by "character." In such circumstances, the true nonconformist is blessed; he is the man who, without being "supercilious," will not give in to demands of the crowd. Blessed, finally, is the man whose faith is not "possessiveness," who does not depend on material or psychological advantages for the self, and who is not limited to the evidence of the senses. He is the man who knows that spiritual victory awaits him. This man, whose eyes are "illumined" by spirit, has seen the light of what Moore regarded as religious truth.

The blessed man is the "hero" of her early poems, coveting nothing that he has let go. He is now, however, a man whose behavior is ethical not only in its conformity to traditional standards but also in specifically religious ways. He accepts the faith expressed in the Bible (Hebrews 11:3) that "the worlds were framed by the word of God, so that things which are seen were not made of things which do appear." As it differs with the principles of the Beats, so the poem differed with fashions in literary criticism. Indeed, Moore says in her lecture "Idiosyncrasy" that the poem was written to combat the "denigration," the smart cynicism that she detected whenever a critic commented upon the presence in a piece of writing of the "gusto" that she thought vital to literary art.

O to Be a Dragon

The fifteen poems brought together in 1959 under the title *O to Be a Dragon* continue the themes of the previous volume. The title poem expresses the wish to have, like the dragon of Chinese legendry, the "power of Heaven"—the ability to infuse the world with moral and spiritual strength without having to give up one's own being. Moore's wish typically was for the ability to adopt such guises as may be necessary for defense of the self and for expression of it.

The remaining fourteen poems discover one or another of her values in such diverse subjects as a chameleon, holidays, and baseball games. Assurance is evident in "I May, I Might, I Must," a short declaration of confidence that first appeared in the Bryn Mawr literary magazine *Tipyn O'Bob* in 1909 under the title "Progress." Moore did not reprint this in any volume before *O to B a Dragon;* that she could revive it after fifty years proves not that there had been no change in her thinking, but rather that in maturity she could safely express the confidence that from a less securely established writer might seem banal. The air of hesitancy, of one talking to herself, conveys the idea of an expression that is being given only after thoughtful consideration.

Another poem from her early years is "To a Chameleon." In a typography suggestive of the way the chameleon might "twine" himself round a grapevine, the poem first addresses the creature and then declares that even firelight reflected by an emerald as "massy" as that of the Dark King (Prester John) could not "snap the spectrum up for food" as the chameleon has done—could not incorporate the varied colors the chameleon is capable of assuming. The emerald is an appropriate jewel for comparison to the greenery in which the chameleon is imagined to be hiding, and the chameleon himself is another in the series of well-defended creatures Moore hailed throughout her career. In his symmetry with nature he represents perfection of being.

Yet another defensive guise is saluted in "A Jellyfish," which describes briefly the "fluctuating charm" of the creature and then reports that, when one approaches it, its motion is that of quivering and so one will refrain. The poem is in its first lines a simple report of a circumstance; but "quivers" and "abandon" in the last two lines give it a degree of emotional impact. At no point does the poet allude to the notion of the jellyfish as the weak, "spineless," or cowardly creature popular symbolism makes of it. That she could successfully flaunt so fixed a conception proves the rigor of her skill.

"Values in Use" is a deft satire on those who recommend specific language but fail to employ it themselves. The piece begins with a seemingly offhand, conversational remark that itself illustrates the point by specifying what the poet liked in the setting of a literary colloquium. The second, third, and fourth stanzas quote and paraphrase recommendations of a speaker urging his listeners to live by values in their daily lives and to write concretely of them. The poet's question at the end of the fourth stanza—"Am I still abstruse?"— implies, of course, that the speaker she is reporting on has failed to exercise his own recommendation. The closing two stanzas cite the comment of a student who remarked that he understood two of the "big" words used, and they conclude quickly that "Certainly the means must not defeat the end." This ending is itself an abstraction, a generalization; but the reader should note the skill with which the poet leads up to it and, for that matter, the deliberately trite wording of it. Moore avoids the effect of a tacked on moral by so shaping her poem that the ending grows out of the body of the work not as a logical conclusion nor as a piece of cleverness but as an inevitably just remark in a meditative dialogue.

Few careers are shorter than that of a major league baseball player; and changes in the geographical distribution of teams in the 1950s took the Brooklyn Dodgers to Los Angeles. The reader of "Hometown Piece for Messrs. Alston and Reese" must therefore be a fan of some standing if he is to remember all the names and teams and incidents that the poem incorporates. Yet, topical though it is, the poem is invigorating. The direction that it is to have the tune of a popular song that mentioned a mockingbird and a brass ring sets the tone of lively if faintly ironic humor. In view of the disappearance of the Dodgers from Brooklyn, there now is a heavier irony; the loss of the tradition-laden team for monetary reasons left a taste of brass in the mouths of the community's ardent fans.

But the main import of the poem was celebration and exhortation. It appeared in a New York newspaper on 3 October 1956 during the World Series, and it is essentially a gently humorous appeal to the Dodgers to "Come on," expressing the heady local patriotism of the fans and incorporating allusions to games of the 1955 and 1956 series and to various players and associated personages, as well as snatches of quotations from newspaper articles. Use of specific names and reference to particular incidents give the poem its air of reality; it is a celebration by one who, so to speak, was there. After citing a noted pitcher's remark that "Everything's getting better and better," the poem further illustrates hometown zest by referring to a humorous salute a Dodger band had ready for visiting tax collectors. The emotional ups and downs of the hopeful fan are reported in a series of stanzas alluding to actual incidents and occasionally slipping into the first person in order to identify poet and reader with the fan; the rhythms, with abrupt shifts in pace and direction, seem to parallel the quick changes in mood of one who follows a lively game closely. Mentions of the superstition of many sports followers, the competence of favorite players, and the "color" and affection of a baseball man who got the club to give the proceeds from a game to a charity, all help build the tribute to the hometown team.

The last two stanzas become slightly more serious, urging the team to overmaster its reputation as a somewhat ridiculous grouping and citing its resources in manpower, tradition, and public support. The poem finds Moore applying the optimism and enthusiasm that she valued to a particular instance, and in turn illustrates the presence of these values in her thinking. If too topical for one not an informed fan, it is spirited fun for such a fan and for the reader who is willing to work carefully through the notes and reread them often enough to become at home with the allusions.

The remark that one player "almost dehorned" the opposition, and the playful direction to the Dodgers to "Take off the goat-horns," properly indicate that the conflict is after all not a very "serious" one. One effect of the poem was to make Moore a widely known poet of the city. Whether they understood it, or even read it, many New Yorkers who had ignored poets all their lives were pleased (as was the Dodgers' front office) with the fact that an artist had paid tribute to the supposed national pastime as carried out in Brooklyn.

A more serious production is "Enough: Jamestown, 1607–1957," a poem inspired by observation of the 350th anniversary of the settlement at Jamestown. In honor of the settlers' ships the *Godspeed, Susan Constant,* and *Discovery,* three United States Air Force jet planes were given the same names and flown nonstop across the Atlantic to Virginia on 13 May 1957. Moore's speaker alludes only briefly to these circumstances, but she explores in detail the difficulties, setbacks, and achievements of the settlers to see whether their accomplishment was, taken in the balance, "enough" to initiate the kind of culture she honors. Carefully naming the ships—partly because she enjoys the quaint moralism of their titles—she remarks on how the confident adventurers found their anticipated paradise "too earthly"—a land then of "pests and pestilence." Eight stanzas detail the colonists' difficulties and cite an incident illustrative of relations with Indians: Princess Pocahontas found that in marriage to a white she surrendered her high status, yet that her situation was "not too tame." The implication seems to be that a judgment on their relations would find good and bad mixed.

Three stanzas then specify some of the flowers representative of the careful beauties of present-day Virginia, a passage reminiscent of "Virginia Britannia." But the scene is again changed; there was no time in early Virginia, we are reminded, for the "French effect," for gardening and rhyming. Remarks upon the paradox that "Marriage, tobacco, and slavery" brought a form of liberty—economic stability and security—conclude, fittingly, that no one knows for sure "what is good."

The conclusion is that what the settlers did was indeed "enough": it was a genuine accomplishment because what material gain was achieved was accomplished by "faith." If "proof" of men's material and ideational expectations for the new country was at the time only "partial," the "present faith" made their settlement nevertheless of significance for us, especially if our faith will "mend" the inadequacies of the heritage the settlers left us. One may note especially the absence of sentimentality: the Jamestown settlers are seen to be greedy enough yet not villainous. The mixture of selfishness and faith that motivated them is acknowledged without debunking or prettifying. As in "The Jerboa," greed is recognized; but humor, specificity, and restraint convey a tolerance enabling the poet to communicate her belief that the moral system indicated by the very names of the ships was wrong insofar as it incorporated greed, but was right insofar as it led to decency of behavior. The 1981 printing drops three stanzas and makes several lesser alterations. The changes speed the pace, but eliminate the observation that the settlers' ships— that is, by implication, something of their hopes—live on in "name-sake" jets.

Faith is also the topic of "Melchior Vulpius," a poem celebrating the composer whose works include an anthem in praise of "conquering faith" in God. The power of such an artist is, we are told, something we must "trust," for it cannot be finally understood though it can be acquired and directed. Such art, at least on the level of ingenuity, is also instanced by construction of automatons with lungs of mouse-skin, here imagined as saying "Hallelujah." We assume that the composer is thought to have received his power of expression from on high; man's abilities to parallel the activities of God—and the enormous difference in respective powers—are indicated by the lines on the automaton: the device is to be respected, yet obviously is far inferior in capacity to the creations of God. Manlike, the composer built from "miniature thunder"; yet, god-like, what he built up were "crescendos antidoting death." If this is a paradox, it is, if not explained, at least celebrated by the declaration that it amounts to "love's signature cementing faith," a love of the artist for the spirit firming the faith of all who hear him.

The restorative power of a work of art is honored in "No Better than 'a withered daffodil,' " originally published in *Art News*. For purposes of the poem, Ben Jonson is imagined as having written in "Slow, Slow, Fresh Fount" that he was in the state indicated by Moore's title. (In Jonson's poem it is "nature's pride" that is said to be a withered daffodil; this pride, however, may be a quality in the speaker of the poem.) At any rate, Moore's first stanza quotes the fine lines in which Jonson compares the feeling of his speaker to the dripping of melting snow. We would expect Moore to reject such a feeling, for she does not, at least in verse, give way to expressions of despair. Here she does say "I too," but immediately relates how the sight of a green French brocade revived her spirits.

She does not communicate this story in the direct fashion of a sermon writer; instead, she gives comparisons that will make the point to our senses—the brocade reminds her of "some lizard in the shade," then of a miniature picture on ivory showing Sir Philip Sidney. These remarks give her strength back to her: "I too," she now remarks, seem to be as "insouciant" as Sidney and "no daffodil," no drooping, melancholy spirit.

Art in its public function and in its individuality are considered in "In the Public Garden," read at an Arts Festival in Boston in June 1958 (earlier titles were first "A Festival," then "Boston"). The situation of the poet as participant in a public salute to the arts calls up the reflections. The first stanza introduces duality, speaking of a festival "for all" taking place near the Harvard campus that has "made education individual." This leads to mention of "fine" individuals in the conversation of an "almost scriptural" Boston taxi driver—one who conforms to the newspaper columnists' portrait of cabmen as sages. The environment's beauties are specified in Moore's usual exact detail: a weathervane, iris, snowdrops. The movement in the passage is backward, from summer to spring and finally winter, an ordering perhaps intended to force the reader's attention upon the details by slightly disrupting his expectation.

After these appreciative mentions of individuals and nature, the theme of gratitude enters in the sixth stanza with a quotation from a hymn heard in King's Chapel. A chapel, we are then told, is like a festival in that it involves an exchange—we deduce the exchange of gratitude for grace in a chapel, of attention or pay for inspiration in a festival; but the poem goes on to cite not such expected reciprocations but rarities, the most "unusual" being "silence." This gift may come, we surmise, in a chapel or in a work of art. At any rate, it is said to be as "unattainable" as freedom, and this leads to yet another statement of Moore's belief that freedom and self-discipline are related. This statement she conveys by quoting President Eisenhower and by citing the determination of inmates of a "transshipment camp" to earn passage to freedom by selling medicinal herbs, a strategy they could not succeed in if they allowed themselves to become ill. Man is, as the hymn said, child to God; but he will live up to this role only if he disciplines the self.

"Well?" the poet pretends to interrupt. Some, she says, will talk on and on without saying why they have come. Having just praised "silence" and self-discipline, she feels an obligation to be brief.

What she is giving us, she says, is neither a madrigal nor a gradual—
it is not to be formal, elaborately artistic, but "grateful." The
gratitude is aroused by the experience of seeing the assemblage "wish
poetry well." Modestly speaking of herself as lacking the "radiance"
romantic tradition assumed poets to have and as commenting quite
unofficially, she says that she can nevertheless be glad that the arts
have "a home and swans"—both a welcoming physical environment
and an aesthetically receptive spirit.

She is "happy," finally, that Art—now capitalized—though admired "in general" on such occasions as the festival, remains "actually personal," the product of the artist. The artist needs, and
here retains, it would seem, "freedom" to express himself, a freedom
consisting in part of a "silence," an absence of demands from the
public. Art has its public function, but this is not to result in
pressures upon the artist; Boston, Harvard, and the arts festival thus
are gracefully praised for affording opportunity for a hearing without
imposing demands. The poem does make use of the conventional
formula for an invited artist's address to a crowd, disclaiming any
thought that the honor is for oneself and expressing gratitude rather
for the honor given to the art. But the conventional here is carefully
explored.

Playful delight in the friendliness, peacefulness, and intelligence
of the musk ox in "The Arctic Ox (or Goat)" shows Moore's admiration for these qualities. The poem celebrates the animal of the
title by detailing his qualities as set down in a magazine article
Moore cited as her source. She followed the article closely, even to
such humorous directions as "Bury your nose in one when [he is]
wet" (said to one who persists in believing the animal to have a
musk-like odor). The article expresses the wish that man make use
of the animals by adjusting his economy to his environment in areas
where conventional agricultural practices are destructive or futile.
But Moore omitted this wish for social betterment; she preferred to
indicate through her celebration of the animal her admiration for
the qualities it represents. The ninth stanza calls to mind her poem
"Rigorists," which remarks upon the salvation of an Eskimo community by the importation of reindeer.

The musk ox embodies many of the qualities that Moore admired
and that she believed result from inner spirit. The kind of spiritual
inspiration she would have liked is defined in "Saint Nicholas," a
poem written for a Christmas edition of the *New Yorker* magazine.

The poem approaches its goal playfully, but purposefully; the first stanza suggests that a welcome Christmas gift would be a chameleon, thus establishing at once the attitude of moderation in desire that we expect of a poet who values restraint, "silence," and self-discipline. The description of the animal is based on a *Life* magazine photograph of a chameleon which, being behind the bars of a cage in the sunshine, appeared to be striped. Each detail is accurate, including the tightly coiled tail and the slight doubt as to whether one should count six or seven stripes. Another desirable gift, the poem continues, would be a garment of musk-ox fibre and a fancy shirt. Such wishes are, if hardly routine, at least within reasonable expectation. To reinforce the point that her desires are not extreme, Moore's speaker in the third stanza declares that she would not want "a trip to Greenland" or to the moon. Let the moon come here and perhaps enable her to garb herself in moonlight—that would be acceptable.

Thought of the moon introduced a note of greater possibility, and the poem moves on to suggest a "yet more rare" desire. Describing Hans von Marées's painting of St. Hubert, the speaker mentions the figure's bowed head and erect form, "tense with restraint." The stance is one she honors. Now she repeats, generalizing slightly, her description of the scene; we are to recall that the St. Hubert of legend was so fond of hunting that he neglected his religious duties until one day he met in the forest a stag who bore in his horns a miraculous crucifix that warned him to reform. Hubert, the story goes, thereafter became a noted churchman. The speaker's overt request is quite in line with the imaginative but modest desires she has thus far expressed. But in the last four lines of the poem she suggests deeper desire. She maintains the restraint: she does not tell Saint Nicholas what she would like, only that he "must have divined" what it would be. We may deduce that she, like the latter-day Hubert, would desire a vision of Christ. Moore will not state this overtly; her "silence," her self-discipline are too taut to permit a declaration that might smack of romantic excess. Yet her understatement is, she knows, fully emotive.

"Saint Nicholas" indicated the love for God that is directly the theme of "For February 14th." The strategy for movement in this work is an address to Saint Valentine, asking him if he would welcome as a gift a poem, a diamond, a plant, or some birds. This, of course, is a witty reversal of the customary Valentine's Day exchange of favors between lovers. The series of suggested gifts ends suddenly with the exclamation that such questioning "is the mark of a pest!" Why, the concluding lines ask, do we think only of "animals," of material benefits? Why do we not think instead of the fact that "the ark did not sink"—of the love God expresses toward man?

Religious love would develop a unity between God and man, but unity of a different sort is the theme of the last two poems of this volume. "Combat Cultural" honors the lessoning obtained from the sight of two ballet dancers enacting a scene of combat though dressed as twin brothers. The "moral" they point to, the ending says wryly, is the need to unify the elements of any "objective" that represents wisdom and ethical behavior. The work of art, we deduce, should unite whatever diversities it may contain. As often, the poem leads up to its objective with a seeming indirectness, beginning with references to various scenes of active creatures leaping or flying, moving to Russian dances and then to Arctic Russian sack wrestling in which the combatants are blanketed together. From seemingly casual suggestions of physical action the poem moves first to the generalized unity of action in a dance, then to the enforced unity of a sack dance, and finally to the ballet scene that suggests most directly the "moral" the speaker draws.

Unity of all men under Christ is an ideal in "Leonardo da Vinci's," a poem based on the painter's famous picture of St. Jerome and the lion. Jerome, we are reminded, was "versed in language"; most of the poem concerns the nonlinguistic but effective symbolism of the lion. In the second and third stanzas the old tale is told of how Jerome supposedly dressed the wounded paw of a lion that thereupon remained as his companion, of Jerome's suspicion that the beast had eaten an ass, and of the disgrace that consequently came to the lion until he retrieved the ass from a company of thieves. The result was the forging of a strong bond between Jerome and the lion; it was so strong, indeed, we are told, that they became "twinned" in "lionship." Leaned but taught by his troubles, Jerome used his talents in language to put together the Vulgate Bible.

The lion, too, left his contributions. In the last two stanzas Moore cites use of him as a sign of the zodiac for early summer and the consequent honoring of him by Egyptians because of his connection with the rise of the Nile. And, the poem remarks, in da Vinci's picture the sun seems to imbue Jerome and the lion; the last stanza appropriately gives the direction "blaze on." We are reminded that the sun shone especially during the zodiacal season of Leo and that in Christian mythology the lion, like the sun, traditionally has been emblematic of the resurrection of Christ. The closing words—directing Haile Selassie, emperor of Ethiopia, to shine on as do picture, saint, and beast—make an ending that is typical for Moore in seeming casual; but it is typical also in having more relevance than may first appear, for Haile Selassie was referred to as the Lion of Judah, a title that, because of the lion symbolism, is now sometimes used for Christ. Haile Selassie represents the afflicted people Moore had already spoken of in such poems as "In Distrust of Merits." Though the emperor later would be viewed as an anachronistic tyrant, when Moore published the poem (1959) he was still a hero to Americans because of his resistance to Mussolini in the 1930s.

Tell Me, Tell Me

Until her health began to fade in the late 1960s, Moore remained an active poet as well as a New York City celebrity. The serious verse of her later years may be characterized as reaffirmation. It continues insistence on the values of courage, independence, silence, and art, and it reasserts need to recognize the invisible within the visible.

Much of Moore's work now, however, was occasional verse, frequently written at the request of an editor or public figure. Even in her more serious pieces, her imagination in the 1960s seemed less intense, appearing in tributes or comments that use her techniques but lack the depth of inspiration that gave rise to her better work. "Granite and Steel," for example, has the manner but not the combination of lightness in touch and wisdom in idea that one notes in "The Plumet Basilisk," "The Jerboa," and "The Mind Is an Enchanting Thing." When the later pieces are serious, they tend to be heavy-footed, lacking the imaginative "feel" that earlier gave Moore empathy with her subject and by means of this unity made implication expressive. What is missing is the "gusto," the delight in experience.

Her next collection of poems appeared in 1966 as *Tell Me, Tell Me*. The 1981 *Complete Poems* prints all eighteen of these pieces, but does not give four short prose essays that were printed with them. Comparing the 1966 and 1981 printings shows that Moore dropped one line from the early version of "Granite and Steel" and made a few lesser changes, none of them of important effect on significance. Continuing her recognition of spirit and insistence on moral values, "Granite and Steel" finds the quality of "probity" exemplified in Brooklyn Bridge, which stands only a few blocks from the poet's longtime home in Brooklyn. To the speaker, the bridge, an "enfranchising cable," and the Statue of Liberty, which stands on shattered chains, dominate the bay. The bridge in its artistry opposes greed, symbolizing mankind's highest capacities and serving in its practicality to overcome the avarice of those who—as a somewhat thorny passage seems to indicate—would put profit ahead of beauty and utility. Stanza 3 celebrates, somewhat in the manner of Hart Crane, the "harmony" of earth and sky, the "radiance" the bridge represents and contributes to. The bridge is, indeed, a "composite span," a meld of the imagined and the achieved and a representation of mankind's aspirations. It is an example of what Moore wished her poems to be.

"Granite and Steel" typically requires the reader to slow down and, as is frequent, also requires that he bring in a bit of factual knowledge about its subject. It is followed in *Tell Me, Tell Me* by the two-page prose consideration of the way a poem states its content, "A Burning Desire to Be Explicit." Reporting two incidents in which her explicitness had been questioned, Moore remarks that though there may be an "element of the riddle" in a poem, most readers may not be "irked by clues to meaning." This assertion is followed by two examples of painters' brief explanations of elements in their work. Examples from her own writing are meant to show that she does not intend either abstraction or philosophy. One should want, she indicates, to use words with passion and to lift the heart (she quotes Faulkner on the latter point, though primly noting that his writing "might not always have done that").

"In Lieu of the Lyre" is Moore's only outrightly feminist poem, a deliberately intricate response—"reflections," the ending styles it—to an invitation in 1965 to send a poem to the *Harvard Advocate*. The guise of the speaker is as one expressing gratitude for the invitation, yet the overall effect is ironic, even satiric. Though "debarred" from Harvard (which at the time did not admit women), the speaker can feel "with fire" at sight of the college's historic campus and also, one deduces, at the smart from what she takes to be the exclusion of members of her gender. The notes identify a

French phrase as a quotation from Madame Boufflers (1711–1786), a writer whose work is discussed in a 1951 article by Dr. Achilles Fang (identified in the notes to "Tom Fool at Jamaica"). The second stanza continues the excessive intricacy; its content amounts to the remark that the speaker is "a too outspoken outraged refugee from clichés." Having amusingly punished the *Advocate*'s young editor and readers with these near-impenetrable observations; the speaker turns in the last two stanzas to the sly suggestion that they might prefer some plain axiom: she cites two elementary statements of physics, and the simple fact that Roebling invented the Roebling cable. "In Lieu of the Lyre" indeed! In lieu of a poem Moore writes a send-up of the university. Other pieces of occasional verse include "Dream," an expression of admiration for Bach; and "Old Amusement Park," a recollection of the "tame-wild" place, of its bustle, and also of the insouciance of employees who would shut up shop in order to chat.

In contrast to the delight in the mind that is celebrated in "The Mind Is an Enchanting Thing" is the despair—humorously rueful, rather than tragic—noted in "The Mind, Intractable Thing." Here the mind is seen as somehow separate from the self, making suggestions that "I" cannot follow. Addressing it as an "imagnifico"— a term Moore apparently compounded from "image" or "imagine" and "magnifico" (which she may have come across in Wallace Stevens's writing), the speaker reflects on two examples of pictures the mind brings to attention—a glen and an Arizona road-runner, both observed in exact detail, and then lists items the mind understands and knows how to deal with, matters that "I" feels she cannot successfully handle. The exclamation "O Zeus and O Destiny!" suggests that the speaker is not seriously disabled by such incompetencies: one may deduce that she is somewhat taken aback by the range of possibilities the mind roams over. Despite even such obstacles as "disparagers, deaths, dejection" the mind continues in its ways; it has made "wordcraft" irresistible to her, is as close to a king over her as any power can be, is, indeed, the possessor of a craft that is intractable because it cannot be controlled and tamed. The mind that is a delight in its operations is also, it seems, fecund and wily in its domination of the self.

A more serious point is raised in "An Expedient—Leonardo da Vinci's—and a Query." Noting that da Vinci worked with patience and a sure memory, that he had a "height" of artistic character that

kept traducers away, and that he followed but did not merely imitate
nature, the speaker asks how after painting his *Leda* he could have
been so dejected that he wondered whether he had accomplished
"anything / at all" (a question that, according to the Kenneth Clark
book Moore cites in her notes, Leonardo frequently asked). The
poem muses: was Leonardo not in fact able to handle the changes
he saw in reality? The lines indirectly assert that the proof of an
artist's greatness is in what he creates, not in his theories. The poem
"W. W. Landor" is another comment on aesthetics, admiring the
English writer who was physically forceful yet so "tender" that when
he threw a man through a window he worried about the violets the
fellow would land on, an accomplished artist who modestly avoided
grand abstractions—a man, that is, after Moore's own heart.

"To a Giraffe" is a reflection on the challenge facing the artist.
Her note shows that Moore had in mind *The Odyssey*, a work that,
in her view, one deduces, sets an unmatchable standard of accomplishment. The speaker first asks whether, if the artist is not to be
personal or literal, and should be innocent, he or she is required to
work always at the highest reach. She finds the idea represented in
the giraffe, an animal that pleasures her because it is "unconver-
sational." This notion causes her to observe that one wrapped up
in the self and its problems can be unbearable even though the self
had the possibility of being exceptional. From this attempted rejection of the overly personal and the self-engrossed the speaker
turns to the thought that consolation for what seem the difficulties
of the artist and others can be found in Homer, who shows a world
that is flawed and conditional, one where "the journey from sin to
redemption" is perpetual, where people are forever imperfect though
forever being redeemed. The quotation that ends the poem is from
Moore's own summary of a scholar's views on *The Odyssey.*

To Moore, a spiritual element unites experiences acrobatic, athletic, and artistic, and it unifies seemingly disparate qualities of
character. It also enables the moral to triumph over the sinful.
"Charity Overcoming Envy" shows the good mastering the evil that
is yoked to it by convincing it that its self-pity is misguided. This
victory shows that it is not necessary to delay hopes for achievement
simply because the ethical may be linked to error by a "Gordian
Knot." The relative standing of the two qualities is indicated by
the fact that Charity rides on an elephant—generally an admirable
creature in Moore's work—but Envy is mounted on a dog. In *Tell*

Me, Tell Me this poem is followed by "Profit Is a Dead Weight,"
a five-page prose urging to moral behavior, an unexpected inhabitant
of a book of poems but one showing Moore's traditional values of
responsibility, sympathy, and courage, and her opposition to greed
and cynicism. The poem concludes that one following such principles will be so popular that she will have no leisure. Moore pro-
tested to me, and others, that people often attempted to take her
over. Slight in build, and known for rectitude, she appealed, as she
recognized, to the sense of solicitude in many readers and in the
nonreading fans whose attention the press was bringing her by the
1960s.

Analogy between the artistic and the athletic serves to suggest
the importance of spirit. Explaining that the title "Blue Bug" is
the name of a polo pony she saw pictured in *Sports Illustrated* (13
November 1961), the speaker draws attention to a kinship between
herself and the pony; the animal recognizes the recognition in her
eye. She won't ask how he got his odd name, she says; she comments
on the intrusiveness of those who pester one with questions (an idea
she also discussed in "Saint Nicholas"). Then, as if interrupting a
conversation, she breaks in abruptly with the declaration that "I've
guessed" and goes on to describe the pony as resembling an artist's
dragonfly in its ability to make quick turns in direction. This
description leads to analogy between the pony's abilities and the
intricacies of a Chinese melody. She remarks that the tune gives an
accurate "version" of the pony's varied movements in polo.

Having found a similarity between herself and the pony and
having also asserted a resemblance between him and works of art,
the speaker climaxes the analogy by "restating" it. Though *polo*
actually comes from the Tibetan word for the ball used in the game,
it looks like a Romance language word, a fact she takes advantage
of to obtain a bit of wordsmanship implying a similarity between
"polo" (she translates this as "I turn"), *"polos"* (plural of a Spanish
word for the polar axis of a spinning object), and the name of the
game. She, the artist, turns on a "pivot" just as do the pony and
the Chinese tune, we are told. The implication is that, diverse as
all these may be, there is a kinship because all turn on a pivot of
spirit. The poem recognizes that the analogy may be "a little elaborate," but explains, in Moore's usual deftly casual manner, that
such a relationship between the idea of revolving and the thought
of a "pastime" was suggested by thought of Odilon Redon, a French

Postimpressionist painter. The painter's name itself must have pleased
Moore by its sounds. And she doubtless approved of his assertions
that once an artist has mastered his language, he should be free to
deal with subjects drawn not only from direct observation but also
from history and poetry. As "Baseball and Writing" found that the
artist and the athlete should "bear down" but "enjoy it," so in "Blue
Bug" it is remarked that the art Redon preferred was a "pastime
that is work." One should have the physical control and the alert
mentality of a Chinese acrobat; the closing stanza particularizes this.

References to a Chinese tune and to a Chinese acrobat have a
general appropriateness in that polo came to the West from the
Orient; they also remind the reader of the admiration and attention
Moore gives Chinese artistry in "Nine Nectarines" and "O to Be a
Dragon." Whether the performer is from China or from Brooklyn,
if he is to be bulwarked for right action by acquiring the powers
of the dragon, he must recognize the spiritual element that gives
unity not only to experiences but also to seemingly disparate qualities of character. "Arthur Mitchell" is only a verse intended for
notes to a dance program, but in celebrating the dancer as one whose
jewel-like mobility both reveals and veils, Moore indicates again
her own desire to be both explicit and armored.

Like writing, dancing is a public art. Baseball, too, requires an
infusion of spirit. The relationships are explored in "Baseball and
Writing," a poem in which one theme is the nature of beauty. The
verse makes use of humorous rhymes ("pedagogy"—"prodigy"),
abrupt shifts in rhythm, and citation of the names of living people
to establish a familiar, conversational tone that reinforces the remark
of the last stanza that one—whether baseball player or, we deduce,
writer—should "bear down" at his work but "Enjoy it." The opening stanza says excitement over writing or baseball is not mere
"fanaticism," though it arouses a "fever" in its "victim."

Bantering about the point, Moore mentions the "Owlman" (her
italics) in the pressbox—a reference to the sportswriters and broad-
casters assigned to night games and to their role as public wisemen.
Several stanzas praise the skills of various baseball players, most of
them New York Yankees. Since we have been warned by the title
and by the first stanza to watch for analogies with writing, we are
likely to read such a remark as "concentrates promote victory" as
significant of Moore's aesthetic theory, though as usual the gener-

alization is grounded in the specifics of a seemingly very different area—in this case, a listing of supposed health foods.

The complexity of Moore's attitudes is indicated by her willingness to link baseball with writing; this linking gives a profundity to such lines as "Pitching is a large subject"—a remark conveying a truth in the light of humor. So too the sixth stanza, listing some of the "imponderables"—the hazards the player faces—notes such actual physical dangers as muscle kinks and spike wounds, yet mentions the pains of celebrity with the hardly serious exclamation "Drat it!" and intermixes play on sounds with its remark that "the Stadium is an adastrium." The stadium—the arena, we assume, of both the athlete and the writer—is the home of "stars," a designation not only of celebrities but also of personages whose values are admirable. Thought of stars leads to the appropriate closing salute to Orion, the symbol of that strength and skill which create the beauty Moore finds in expert performance whether in the arena or on the page. The techniques in "Baseball and Writing" are much the same those in "Hometown Piece for Messrs. Alston and Reese." But Moore was deliberately more topical in the poem written for publication at the height of a World Series fever, and the allusions in it to players now half-forgotten are something of a chore for the reader to master. In "Baseball and Writing," in contrast, the topical allusions, though sufficient to ground the poem in particulars, hardly matter to the "story."

In the prose passage "A Burning Desire to Be Explicit" Moore cited her poem "To Victor Hugo of My Crow Pluto" as an example of narrative meant to make a practical observation, rather than to make an abstract point: the crow was a real one, not a symbol or a merely generalized bird. In *Tell Me, Tell Me* she printed before this poem the two-and-a-half-page prose commentary "My Crow, Pluto—a Fantasy." The passage tells how Pluto, a crow who lived in a park about a block from Moore's Brooklyn apartment, adopted her, bringing her trophies and eating food she herself liked. Moore defends crows as useful birds, comments amusingly on his feeding, and on his fondness for her desk and typewriter, and reports that she eventually set him free in the Connecticut woods. Though the prose speaks of the poem as a "two-syllable-line, two-line stanza," Moore in fact has from two to five syllables per line; most readers will see it as a *jeu d'esprit*. The "fantasy" of the title seems to mean only that keeping the bird about her for some weeks or months was an entertaining but impractical act: he belonged, she observes, in the wilds where she eventually released him.

Though it is as playful as the prose, the poem intimates a theme of salvation as it remarks that the speaker released the bird because it had even when walking the look of one who wears wings. The tone is affectionate; the verse makes use of a short line, includes much alliteration and repetition of such sounds as "tuttuto/vagabondo," and thymes throughout on *u* and *o* sounds. (In the essay Moore says that she addressed the bird alternately as Plato or Pluto, depending on the vowel sounds in preceding words.) All this works together to give comic effect. This effect is heightened by use of "esperanto madinusa," much of the last two thirds of the poem being in this idiom that, the essay says, she used in talking to the bird; she furnishes with the poem a word list for "those who might not resent" it.

She tells us with mock seriousness for four of the brief stanzas that the crow is a "true Plato" because he meets Victor Hugo's description as a creature that always seems to possess talents superior to those an unimaginative observer of its pigeon-toed walk might see. The poet recognized the bird's ability to speak and, as she remarks in the essay, his competence at petty thievery. These talents presumably made him worth money to her, but she declares that she lives in the belief that profit is a deadweight; she refuses to profit from her avian friend. Thus, though the bird was a jewel to her, she recognized his essential nature as a free spirit and let him go. The poem is another of Moore's expressions of the need to recognize spirit beneath appearances. It is also, unfortunately, one of Moore's infrequent lapses into doggerel.

The title of "Rescue with Yul Brynner" and the note of explanation that the actor was a special consultant to a United Nations commissioner of refugees direct us to see the poem as yet another exploration of the themes of refuge and rescue. As often, Moore begins indirectly, here with praise of the Budapest Symphony and shamefaced remarks on how as "too slow a grower" she did not recognize the difficulties the orchestra worked under when its members were displaced. In the ninth line the poem jumps abruptly to direct comments upon the number of refugees adrift after World War II, the kindness of Canadians who agreed to accept some who were not in good health, and the virtues of Brynner as a visitor to the refugee camps. Allusions to Brynner's guitar and his cloth cap and to his conversations with refugees come from the pictures and text of his book *Bring Forth the Children* (1960); references to him as regal allude to his starring role in the play *The King and I*.

Though flying from camp to camp like a bird, Brynner, the poem says, was not "feathering himself" but instead was showing sincere concern with the plight of the war victims. Picturing him as "twin" to a dancer in *The King and I* and in the moving picture based on it, and thus an enchanter, the poem moves in the last stanza first to a series of staccato notations of his behavior on his inspection trip, then to a contrast between the reality he dealt with in the refugee camps and the glamor of the palace in the drama, and finally to lines praising his deeds as a Christian by punning on the similarity between his first name and the term Yule for the Christmas season. In his actions, he had become now a true king, not just a theatrical one; and he was truly Christian in behavior, not just a man whose name had accidental similarity to a term for the season of Christ's birth. One must add that there is more admiration than poetry in this piece, though it is a heartfelt tribute.

Salvation is also the theme in "Carnegie Hall: Rescued," a poem exulting in the success of the campaign to save New York's famous concert hall from the wrecking crews. This poem draws on a *New Yorker* magazine account of efforts by Isaac Stern, the renowned violinist, to save the hall; but the material, including some of that in quotation marks, is Moore's own. The poem honors Stern in various ways. Since his name in German means "star," she hails him as "Mr. Star." She also refers to him as Diogenes, the Greek philosopher who supposedly went about with a lantern hunting amongst his fellow citizens for one honest man. She makes the appellation "Saint Diogenes," the "Saint" of course being an honorific. The second stanza, in remarking that the hall "became (becomes)" a "stronghold" for music, seems to be referring to the fact that that hall had long served that function and now will do so again. Perhaps it also suggests the secondary meaning of "becomes"—the hall, though graceless enough, has by long use come to be almost a shrine, and thus a becoming partner to the artistry it houses. The poem's instruction to stress the "ne" in "Carnegie" is properly playful, and wittily parallels the emphasis on music. Also appropriately informal, as a song of exultant triumph may well be, are allusions to the founder as "Andrew C." and to one of the men who helped save the hall, Frederick W. Richmond, as "Mr. R." Their work, we are told, has staved off the menace of real-estate developers who are left cowering like newborn infants. Stanzas 6 and 7 comment that those who demolish worthwhile architectural "glory" are as wrong as the Venetian who did not obey his city's instructions to garb himself decorously in order to present a proper pattern for children to follow. Mentioning a French writer's statement that in youth he dreamed of glory, the poem asks if we must put references to this quality in the past tense; does not that dream find expression in the "glittering" triumph of the campaign to save Carnegie Hall? That musicians have continued to use the hall demonstrates the need for it. This brings up the thought of the praises that "dog" the performer, introducing once again the idea of Diogenes (who is said to have once remarked sarcastically that his title was "dog"). The poem ends with praise of the "glittering" violinist as one who came to the rescue "as if you'd heard yourself performing"—a remark meant not as an implication that the violinist is egotistic, but as an assertion that Stern devoted his full energies to the campaign, as might a man who had strong self-interest.

Salvation takes various guises. How the poet who believes in need for self-discipline and restraint may avoid self-centeredness that would lead her to violate unity of expression is the problem of "Tell Me, Tell Me." Excessive individualism may lead one to "obliterate continuity," to "set/flatness on some cindery pinnacle." Thought of a pinnacle leads to the memory of a diamond rosette that appeared, because of its geometric workmanship, to be the product of a "passion for the particular" suited to a Henry James or to a Beatrix Potter. In such a passion, we discover, lies the "refuge" from egocentricity. We may recall that egocentricity means not only ordinary self-centeredness but also the belief that things exist only in the mind, a belief from which particularism will save one. Faith in the existence of a realm of spirit does not for Moore deny existence of a realm of "objects."

Joint allusion to James and to Miss Potter is a playful but not merely antic conjunction. The third stanza quotes from James's autobiography about what he termed the "wholesome" avoidance of excessively "literal" elements in his education. Moore uses his phrases in lines describing the mice of Miss Potter's story of the tailor of Gloucester. The tailor, charged with the duty of cutting a coat for the mayor, despite weariness, cut the pieces for a masterpiece (of cerise, we are reminded—a color reminiscent of the diamond rosette). He was unable to complete the work because he fell ill, but the mice he had saved from his cat finished it for him. The tailor thus was "rescued" from poverty and despair, and we recall the cry for refuge that opened the poem as Moore announces in the fourth stanza that she is going "to flee."

She will do this by "engineering strategy"; but ironic reference to such strategy as "the viper's traffic-knot" seems to imply that, like the viper in Aesop's tale who injured himself by his own bite, traffic engineers have only helped knot up the flow of vehicles. What she would flee to are "metaphysical" delights. The way to this refuge, it appears, lies not only in clinging to particulars of experience; it also lies in that silence Moore admires. Might one tell himself, she asks, to hush up? At first she suggests this request might be in French, and playfully puns on R.S.V.P.; but she then turns serious to remark that courtesy hardly makes sense to one who seriously needs to escape from "verbal ferocity." This latter phrase is an apt summation of the faults she suggested in the first stanza; but she avoids letting it serve as climax by attaching with a semicolon the remark that she is "perplexed."

The puzzlement, we deduce, is over how to remain free from egocentricity; the proper strategy, she now recognizes, is "deference"—a word she first quotes to show its status as an ideal and then uses without quotation marks to indicate acceptance of it as a practical tactic. Useful deference, one that defends, requires respect for the particulars of experience and a willingness to present one's response to these particulars—a poem—without the "verbal ferocity" aroused by "egocentricity."

Playfully conceding that there may be difficulty in following her shifts of thought, Moore presents the final stanza in the guise of an appended précis. It is in actuality a conclusion growing directly out of the materials. Because she is in a plight somewhat analogous to that of Miss Potter's tailor, the poem in making use of his experience is biographical. The tale of the tailor "ended captivity," she tells us, in "two senses." As an event, it released the tailor from despair; as a story, it by its example "rescued" one reader—the poet herself—from "being driven mad by a scold." The tailor was concerned not

so much about his own health as about his commission. Reading
of him caused her to focus on her work and thus saved her from
herself—from the faults of egocentricity.

"Saint Valentine," another of the less-than-wholly-serious poems
of Moore's late career, suggests that tokens distributed as valentines
should have names beginning with V. After giving possible examples, it concludes that verse would indeed be appropriate. Yet,
it adds, a merely written valentine is only as the vintage to the
vine: as the vine is the origin of the grape and its wine, so love is
the motive for the valentine. Valentine verse, then, might "confuse
itself with fate," might, as a sign of love, be a declaration of one's
destiny. In *Tell Me, Tell Me* the poem is followed by the three-page
prose statement "Subject, Predicate, Object." This passage gives
certain of Moore's preferences in style and technique and some of
her attitudes toward verse-writing. The remarks make it obvious
that one of her fundamental drives—perhaps *the* fundamental one—
was great delight in use of words.

The concluding poem in *Tell Me, Tell Me* is "Sun," a piece that
first appeared in 1916 as "Fear Is Hope"; reprinting of it indicates
that Moore still agreed with its point—and suggests caution in
attempts to divide her work into neat periods. The theme in "Sun"
is spiritual resurrection. Quoting John Skelton's "Upon a Dead
Man's Head," that no one may hide from death, the poem says that
this "truth" is not adequate for "us"—for us of freer faith, perhaps,
but also for all who want death to bring with it a purification. The
poem then turns to address the sun, recalling its function as an
emblem of Christ's resurrection and hailing it as a splendor from
the Orient, a "fiery topaz" that shone through the hand of one who
tried to quench it. It is here to stay, we are told, and the second
stanza declares in a vivid figure that "holiday" (derived from "holy
day," we recall) and "day of wrath" shall be one because together

> . . . wound in a device
> of Moorish gorgeousness, round glasses spun
> to flame as hemispheres of one
> great hour-glass dwindling to a stem. . . .

All time, and all times, that is, will be mystically one under the
knowledge of the meaning of resurrection. The poem ends with an
appeal to the sun to blaze against disbelief, to conquer the "insur-

gent" who do not as yet accept belief. Moore's typical poem has wit and intensity presented as thoughtful meditation, often as a carefully worked out progression-by-juxtaposition. But in "Sun" her stance is appropriately lyrical.

Last Poems

The 1981 *Complete Poems* ends with nine poems under the heading "Hitherto Uncollected," and five of the translations from La Fontaine. The nine "uncollected" poems are chosen from the sixteen that Craig S. Abbott's *Bibliography* lists as appearing from 1960 through 1970. The first of the nine, "Avec Ardeur," salutes "gusto"— here given the French designation "ardeur" (that Moore valued the expression "Sentir avec ardeur" [to feel with ardor] appears in both "In Lieu of the Lyre" and "Tom Fool at Jamaica"). The poem was first printed in 1962 as "Occasionem cognosce" (an opportunity for learning), later as "I've Been Thinking," and finally with its present title and an added dedication to Ezra Pound (who had translated the French poem from which Moore borrows the expression "Avec Ardeur" and who had of course supported her throughout her career).[1] The speaker remarks playfully on certain word choices and combinations that Moore would avoid; she concedes ruefully, however, that she is still trapped by such "word diseases." A second set of remarks is on the matter of quantity in verse. The speaker concludes that such comments are "not verse" but that she is at least sure of one principle: that nothing mundane is divine and nothing divine is mundane. Moore, it appears, was reaffirming the principle that real toads must inhabit imaginary gardens.

"Love in America—" declares that the passion for love should be engulfing the country, and should be sustained not as the Minotaur was—the monster of Greek legendry was fed a maiden every year— but by "tenderness." This quality comes from the person who is noble in action and neither too proud nor too self-effacing. These rather flat remarks conclude with a line that repeats the word "Yes" four times, the last time in italics—an attempt at giving a bit of *ardeur* to a statement that is essentially prosaic.

"Tippoo's Tiger" tells of a sultan in eighteenth-century India whose luxuries were (as Elizabeth Phillips has observed) as grossly resplendent as those of the aristocrats in "The Jerboa."[2] Among his possessions was a "curious automaton," a device showing a man killed by a tiger as miniature organ pipes give off inhuman groans. The automaton and the rest of the ruler's possessions were taken by the conquering British. Understanding of this incident's significance awaits "a tiger-hearted bard," the poem's ending observes. The speaker, however, will give one conclusion, the morally triumphant assertion that the great losses Tippoo imposed on the British cannot make up for the loss of his own life in the struggle. Phillips applies the moral to U. S. conduct in the Vietnam war. There is no need to make so specific an application: Tippoo may represent any authority figure who rides the tiger of greed until it turns on and devours him.

Moore's prominence and the public perception of her as a nature poet because of her fondness for animals led her to a leading role in the effort to preserve the tree saluted in "The Camperdown Elm." The tree, planted in Prospect Park in Brooklyn in 1872, draws the speaker's praise as one that causes her to think of poets and painters of the past and of the trees of Paris. (The verse appeal had one unusual recognition: the New York City Department of Parks published it as a leaflet in 1968). "Mercifully" is intended as a graceful salute to the power of music to make the speaker forget disgust at the pretentious and the impercipient; the ending lines, however, are a bit thorny, avoiding danger of relaxation into too easy a rhythm but becoming awkward.

"Reminiscent of a Wave at the Curl" reminds us that Moore preferred direct assertion of the observable to the large abstraction, citing possible grand comments on the playful warfare between two kittens and then noting that the "expert" would say only "Rather hard on the fur." As she would avoid the pretentious and the abstract, so Moore would avoid controversy and the choleric: in "Enough" her speaker avers that to stand for truth is "enough," is all one is obliged to do. There is no requirement, it appears, that we argue with, or go out of our way to tolerate, bad taste and pestering. One who stands for truth will exercise discretion, the quality Moore's speaker finds illustrated in the painting by Magritte that is discussed in the poem "The Magician's Retreat." The painting shows a small house or hut at night with a "yellow glow" showing through a shutter and a blue glow from a lamp over the front door; the scene is complete in itself, is "consummately plain"— an example of the unpretentious reality, the "silence," that Moore favored. But this, of course, is not quite enough: the painting also shows rising behind the hut a "black tree mass" that, though larger than the street scene and done with "definiteness," is "above all" (a pun here) discreet. The tree mass gives a necessary suggestion that there is more in experience than the works of mankind, but this element is nevertheless not to overwhelm. Discretion suggests, it appears, a balancing of elements.

"Prevalent at One Time," separately published in the fall of 1970, was the last of Moore's verse to appear during her lifetime. Perhaps because it comes at the end of *Complete Poems* it is tempting to read into it strong significance. And it does, in fact, support a reading that sees it as a declaration of the "insouciance" Moore admired. The speaker declares that she has always desired a gig, a light horse-drawn carriage for one person, and also a tiger-skin rug for her dog—"the whole thing," meaning both gig and rug, one assumes, to be "glossy black"—perhaps the expected color for a gig but certainly not for such a rug. She, the speaker concludes, is "no hypochondriac." One gathers that Moore's speaker has in mind the approach of death, symbolized by blackness, and is declaring that she does not fear it.

Chapter Six
The Critics' Views

Moore, the poet of delight, understood aesthetics and ethics to be united. In her universe there is as much of the invisible as the visible. Her delight, insouciance, and silence are grounded in assurance that though danger is always present there is nevertheless reason for hope. Her hero therefore perceives the rock crystal thing to see, the "confusion" of the seen and the unseen, both the real toad and the imaginary garden. Asked in 1952 to remark on whether it is "nonsense to talk of a typical American poem," she remarked that she does not see how one can speak of a typically American poem, that Americans achieve poetry not by some species of literary nationalism but by drawing on universal sources, on "depth of experience, imagination, and 'ear.' "[1]

Until the late 1970s, however, her reputation as literary artist was mixed. Throughout her career she had the encouragement and support of her fellow modernists, especially of Pound, Williams, Eliot, and Stevens. Her work also drew the admiration of critics associated with these figures, such men as Yvor Winters, Kenneth Burke, R. P. Blackmur, and Morton Dauwen Zabel. She won most of the major literary prizes and, in good part because of her writing on the Brooklyn Dodgers and other features of New York City life, even became well known in the media.

Moore did not live in an ambience of unremitting praise, however. Long regarded as exceedingly difficult, her poems did not appear before a relatively broad public until the *New Yorker* began to accept them in the late 1940s. Editors of college anthologies began to include them only in the 1950s; in that period the most common choice was "In Distrust of Merits" because academic liberals approved of its sociopolitical rhetoric. Both women and men gave occasional outright dispraise. Like the other modernists, she brought out her work when most readers and critics were still in the grip of romantic notions about what constitutes poetry. Moreover, there was an expectation that a woman writer would be obviously emotional: Edna St. Vincent Millay and H.D. were approved; Moore, seemingly rational and objective, was suspect. Early strong objections came from Margaret Anderson of the *Little Review* and Harriet Monroe of *Poetry*, both of whom doubted that Moore was a poet at all.[2] Men were equally guilty, Louis Untermeyer, for example, declaring in 1923 that "she is not, in spite of the pattern of her lines, a poet."[3] Such dispraise continued into the 1970s: Emily Stipes Watts in *The Poetry of American Women* (1977) wrote that Moore's reputation was fading and that her poetry "will ultimately be unacceptable."[4]

Her reputation with her fellow modernists nevertheless remained high. In the 1960s books on her work made it apparent that it was not after all "difficult" for the reader who will slow down to read attentively and thoughtfully. Moore was aware of her reputation as a writer of the impenetrable, and occasionally remarked on it; looking over my copy of the 1951 *Collected Poems*, in which I had written perhaps more words of notes and interpretation than there are words in the poems, she wrote on the flyleaf "Publish the critical notes, Mr. Engel." My 1964 book, like the books by George W. Nitchie (1969) and Donald Hall (1970), presents readings of the poems, a necessary first step, given the then prevailing notion that only the esoteric dared approach a Moore poem. By the 1970s there was growing awareness that Moore is readable after all. The availability of her "papers" and the rise of the feminist movement increased scholarship, and a second stage of critical treatment began with the appearance of books arguing various theses about Moore's work.

Though, as I write, the feminist movement is highly active in literary criticism, no study giving a specifically feminist interpretation of Moore's work has appeared. Some of the women who have written on Moore in the 1970s and 1980s show touches of feminist views—a tendency to look askance at those of us they lump together as "male critics" is noticeable—but the theses of their books do not rest on feminist assumptions. Moore herself defended the interests and abilities of her gender, but was by no means a "radical feminist." While teaching in Carlisle, Pennsylvania, she distributed suffrage literature and wrote for a suffrage newspaper. Throughout her life she maintained friendship with Bryher, and commented from time to time on the work and careers of H.D. (a fellow student at Bryn Mawr) and Sara Teasdale (another native of St. Louis). She showed recognition of the enforced disabilities of women in her appraisal of M. Carey Thomas of Bryn Mawr, an appraisal that is strong because it is objective rather than sentimental or exclamatory. But her relationships with both women and men were usually professional.

She sought the approval of the leading American poets of her day; it happened that she judged these to be Stevens, Williams, Pound, and Eliot. She remarked, indeed, that "here in America not more than two, or perhaps three, women have even *tried* to write poetry."[5] (The two she had in mind were, one may be sure, Dickinson and herself; mention of a possible third was probably meant only to disarm the critic). Watts spoke for those readers, both female and male, among them some feminists, who still accept the notion that a woman whose work is not declaratively emotional is unwomanly. That view may be fading. In the 1970s and 1980s several women, as well as a number of men, have written thoroughly appreciative studies. In the long run, her work will surely rank with that of the four male poets with whom she compared herself.

Meanwhile, scholarship has not yet given us a sufficient base for Moore studies. We need, for one, works sophisticated enough to recognize that Moore, though no doubt, like most of us, "nice," did not wear a halo. Critics and other readers have an impression of saintliness that comes from early remarks by William Carlos Williams and also from the poet's austere life and her advocacy of moral principle. Yet her papers show that, for example, she was as vicious toward Eleanor and Franklin Roosevelt in the 1930s as any Hearst editorial writer; in a notebook entry dated 19 January 1933 she even wrote that the Roosevelts were responsible for what she saw as an increase in swearing by America's "babes." And she could bear a grudge for a lifetime. In 1962, nearly forty years after the event, she told me, with anger in voice and bearing, that Hemingway had been drunk when he called her up one night to complain about her rejection of his submissions to the *Dial* (it was the drunkenness, not the complaint, that irked her), and that when Wallace Stevens came to dinner with Hemingway in Florida, the poet was "shocked" to discover that his host had picked up a couple of women in a bar to spend the evening with them. Moore was certainly no salon gossip, but she did at times let moralism affect professional judgment.

Criticism and scholarship have assisted understanding. But we need biographies, editions of material from the poet's papers, and, above all, a variorum edition of the poems. Only with these publications will we have a sufficient and readily available base for understanding the work of this great modernist poet.

Notes and References

Preface

1. Moore had proposed chronological order in *Selected Poems*, but accepted Eliot's suggestion for what he termed a "re-shuffle" (T. S. Eliot, letter to Moore, 20 June 1934); Moore and Eliot exchanged suggestions on the order for the 1951 volume (Eliot, letter to Moore, 30 June 1950, and Moore, letter to Eliot, 4 August 1950). The correspondence is in the Rosenbach Museum & Library.

Chapter One

1. "Religion and the Intellectuals," *Partisan Review* 17 (February 1950):137–38.
2. Bonnie Costello, *Marianne Moore: Imaginary Possessions* (Cambridge: Harvard University Press, 1981), 65–70.
3. Moore and Monroe did not see eye to eye. Monroe's relations with Moore and other modernists are discussed in Patricia Willis, *Marianne Moore: Vision into Verse* (Philadelphia: Rosenbach Museum & Library, 1987), 13, 16—17. Moore's later opinion is summed up in a notebook entry for 2 November 1932: "Miss Monroe: she has feeling for some kinds of scholarship but she has no feeling for genius" (Rosenbach).
4. On the significance of the *Dial* experience for Moore, see discussions in Willis, *Marianne Moore*, 13–21, and in Taffy Martin, *Marianne Moore: Subversive Modernist* (Austin: University of Texas Press, 1986), 44–54.

Chapter Two

1. Costello, *Marianne Moore*, 65.
2. Moore, indeed, told Kimon Friar and John Malcolm Brinnin that the lines refer to an incident when she found herself annoyed by a man blocking the view. See their textbook *Modern Poetry, British and American* (New York: Appleton-Century-Crofts, 1951), 523.
3. Costello, *Marianne Moore*, 81–95.

Chapter Four

1. Reviews following the appearance of the *Fables* translation are listed in Eugene P. Sheehy and Kenneth A. Lohf, compilers, *The Achievement of Marianne Moore* (New York: New York Public Library, 1958), 36.

Helen Vendler's view is in "Marianne Moore," in *Marianne Moore,* edited by Harold Bloom (New York: Chelsea House, 1987), 86.

Chapter Five

1. Willis, *Marianne Moore: Vision into Verse,* 88–89.
2. Elizabeth Phillips, *Marianne Moore* (New York: Frederick Ungar, 1982), 221.

Chapter Six

1. Balachandra Rajan, ed., *Modern American Poetry* (New York: Roy, 1952), 182–83.
2. See Margaret Anderson, ed., *The Little Review Anthology* (New York: Hermitage House, 1953), 187–88.
3. Louis Untermeyer, *American Poetry Since 1900* (New York: Henry Holt, 1923), 363.
4. Emily Stipes Watts, *The Poetry of American Women from 1632 to 1945* (Austin: University of Texas Press, 1977), 165.
5. "A Letter from Kathleen Raine," in Tambimuttu, T., ed., *Festschrift for Marianne Moore's Seventy-Seventh Birthday by Various Hands* (New York: Tambimuttu & Mass, 1964), 111.

Selected Bibliography

PRIMARY SOURCES

1. Poetry

Poems. London: Egoist Press, 1921
Observations. New York: Dial Press, 1924
Selected Poems. With an Introduction by T.S. Eliot. New York: Macmillan, 1935.
The Pangolin and Other Verse. London: Brendin, 1936.
What Are Years. New York: Macmillan, 1941.
Nevertheless. New York: Macmillan, 1944.
Collected Poems. New York: Macmillan, 1951.
Like a Bulwark. New York: Viking Press, 1956.
O to Be a Dragon. New York: Viking Press, 1959.
The Arctic Ox. London: Faber and Faber, 1964.
Tell Me, Tell Me: Granite, Steel, and Other Topics. New York: Viking Press, 1967.
The Complete Poems of Marianne Moore. New York: Macmillan and Viking, 1967.
The Complete Poems of Marianne Moore [posthumous]. Edited by Clive Driver and Patricia C. Willis. New York: Macmillan and Viking, 1981.

2. Prose and Miscellaneous

The Complete Prose of Marianne Moore. Edited by Patricia C. Willis. Philadelphia: Rosenbach Museum & Library, 1986.
A Marianne Moore Reader. New York: Viking Press, 1959.
Predilections. New York: Viking Press, 1955.

3. Translations

The Fables of La Fontaine. New York: Viking Press, 1954.
Rock Crystal: A Christmas Tale, by Adalbert Stifter *(Bunte Steine).* With Elizabeth Mayer. New York: Pantheon Books, 1945.

The scholar will need to consult the reading diaries, correspondence, and other Moore papers at the Rosenbach Museum & Library in

Philadelphia. Additional correspondence is in the Beinecke Library
at Yale University.

SECONDARY SOURCES

1. Articles

Bloom, Harold, editor. *Marianne Moore*. New York: Chelsea House, 1987.
Articles by the editor and, among others, Hugh Kenner, Marie Bor-
roff, Helen Vendler, and Bonnie Costello.

"Marianne Moore" issue, *Quarterly Review of Literature* 4 (1948). Contains
a variety of appreciations and articles, including pieces by William
Carlos Williams, Elizabeth Bishop, Wallace Stevens, Cleanth Brooks,
and others.

Tomlinson, Charles, editor. *Marianne Moore: A Collection of Critical Essays.*
Englewood Cliffs, N.J.: Prentice-Hall, 1969. Comments by Moore
herself and statements by, among others, Ezra Pound, T. S. Eliot,
William Carlos Williams, Kenneth Burke, R. P. Blackmur, Hugh
Kenner, and Wallace Stevens.

2. Books

Costello, Bonnie. *Marianne Moore: Imaginary Possessions*. Cambridge, Mass.:
Harvard University Press, 1981. Argues that Moore wanted to be
faithful to the "confusion" of the real while attempting to convey
reality in organized poems.

Hadas, Pamela White. *Marianne Moore: Poet of Affection*. Syracuse, N.Y.:
Syracuse University Press, 1977. Emphasizes Moore's "moral fastidiousness."

Hall, Donald. *Marianne Moore: The Cage and the Animal*. New York:
Pegasus, 1970. Sees Moore's restraint as a disciplining of emotion,
a discipline required by her perception of danger in existence.

Martin, Taffy. *Marianne Moore: Subversive Modernist*. Austin: University of
Texas Press, 1986. Reads Moore as anticipating postmoderns by
undermining the stability of language and observing fragmentation
in experience.

Nitchie, George W. *Marianne Moore: An Introduction to the Poetry*. New
York: Columbia University Press, 1969. Reads the poems as "an
aspect of the moral intelligence of our times."

Phillips, Elizabeth. *Marianne Moore*. Primarily a reading of individual
poems. Draws on the 1967 *Complete Poems* and relies on Stapleton for
information from the Rosenbach papers.

Schulman, Grace. *Marianne Moore: The Poetry of Engagement.* Urbana: University of Illinois Press, 1986. Studies poems to reveal how Moore's creativity "rises from the subtle dialect between freedom and repression."

Slatin, John M. *The Savage's Romance: The Poetry of Marianne Moore.* University Park: Pennsylvania State University Press, 1986. Focuses on the work of Moore's first two decades to show how she responded to what he sees as a sense of isolation at the core of her sense of self.

Stapleton, Laurence. *Marianne Moore: The Poet's Advance.* Princeton: Princeton University Press, 1978. The first book to make extensive use of the Rosenbach papers, this is notable for close observation of Moore's rhythms and diction. Seeing the poems as "a courageous act of self-exploration," it makes the unusual argument that the poetry of Moore's last decades is an advance beyond the work of the early decades that most readers prefer.

Willis, Patricia C. *Marianne Moore: Vision into Verse.* Philadelphia: The Rosenbach Museum & Library, 1987. Meant to serve as a catalog of the Moore exhibition mounted in 1987 at a number of libraries in observance of the centenary of the poet's birth. Gives brief but cogent introductory material followed by information and photographs relevant to thirty-three of the poems.

3. Reference Sources

Abbott, Craig S. *Marianne Moore: A Descriptive Bibliography.* Pittsburgh: University of Pittsburgh Press, 1977. A thorough study, listing separate publications, first-appearance contributions to books, other contributions to books, poems in periodicals, letters, drawings, recordings, and translations.

Lane, Gary. *A Concordance to the Poems of Marianne Moore.* New York: Haskell House, 1972. Useful for comparing uses of words and terms among Moore's various writings.

Sheehy, Eugene P., and K. A. Lohf, compilers. *The Achievement of Marianne Moore: A Bibliography, 1907–1957.* New York: New York Public Library, 1958. Superseded in most respects by the Abbott bibliography, but still useful for lists of articles and reviews.

Index